Lyle Estill

small is possible
life in a local economy

NEW SOCIETY PUBLISHERS

11-08
18 —

CATALOGING IN PUBLICATION DATA:
A catalog record for this publication is available from
the National Library of Canada.

Cover design by Diane McIntosh.
Cover Images: Upper photo (Bees/flower) © Debbie Roos, North Carolina
Cooperative Extension, www.growingsmallfarms.org
Lower image: istock. Interior map © Stayce Leanza.

Printed in Canada.
First printing April 2008.

Paperback ISBN: 978-0-86571-603-2

Inquiries regarding requests to reprint all or part of *Small is Possible*
should be addressed to New Society Publishers at the address below.

To order directly from the publishers, please call toll-free (North America)
1-800-567-6772, or order online at www.newsociety.com

Any other inquiries can be directed by mail to:

New Society Publishers
P.O. Box 189, Gabriola Island, BC V0R 1X0, Canada
(250) 247-9737

New Society Publishers' mission is to publish books that contribute in
fundamental ways to building an ecologically sustainable and just society, and
to do so with the least possible impact on the environment, in a manner that
models this vision. We are committed to doing this not just through education,
but through action. This book is one step toward ending global deforestation
and climate change. It is printed on Forest Stewardship Council-certified acid-
free paper that is **100% post-consumer recycled** (100% old growth forest-free),
processed chlorine free, and printed with vegetable-based, low-VOC inks,
with covers produced using FSC-certified stock. Additionally, New Society
purchases carbon offsets based on an annual audit, operating with a carbon-
neutral footprint. For further information, or to browse our full list of books and
purchase securely, visit our website at: www.newsociety.com

NEW SOCIETY PUBLISHERS
www.newsociety.com

Advance Praise for

Small is Possible

Think local self-reliance is far-fetched in a flat world? Lyle Estill's *Small Is Possible* shows how it's being done for food, housing, energy, finance, health care, and just about everything else communities care about. A seasoned ~~entrepren~~ ~~~~~ ~~~~~ social innovator, Estill tell~~~~~ insightful, and practical. F~~~~~ for community organizer~~~~~

— Michael Shuma~~~~~
How Local Busin~~~~~

Community is quickly emerging as the most important word in the environmental lexicon — and for a society that's focused so squarely on individualist consumerism, it's not the easiest concept to really understand. Here's a real-life, warts-and-all description of how to get things going back in the direction of neighborliness. I found it immensely hopeful.

— Bill McKibben, author of *The Bill McKibb~~~~~*

Reading these storie~~~~~ economy. Estill has ~~~~~ interdependent local~~~~~ a healthy environme~~~~~ shows us the possibi~~~~~ while losing nothing.~~~~~ new economy.

—

This is a wonderful, often funny, and inspiring book. Lyle Estill weaves a tapestry of stories of local people and places that, taken together, begin to form the outlines of sustainable, self-reliant communities united by the desire to cooperate for the common good. *Small is Possible* offers hope and encouragement to those engaged in the difficult but rewarding task of reviving communities that have been devastated by globalization, corporate greed, and apathy. Creating strong, caring, local communities offers one of life's biggest adventures — and opportunities.

— Greg Pahl, author of *The Citizen-Powered Energy
Handbook: Community Solutions to a Global Crisis*

Lyle Estill paints a loving and evocative picture of a community in which small is not only possible, but also transformative.

— Andrea Reusing, Owner/Chef of
The Lantern restaurant in Chapel Hill

Small is Possible is an excellent book brimming with hope. In the Age of Energy transformation, the innovative people of Chatham County show that it is easily possible to reduce their footprints and live joyous lives. This fun book will help many communities across our nation by providing necessary leadership at a crucial time in our history.

— Dr. Reese Halter, TV Host,
Founder of Global Forest Science

Meeting local needs with local resources, employing local people. We've been a neighbor (next door county) of Estill's for many years, and we are constantly looking over our shoulders, trying to keep up with those folks in Chatham Co. We invite you to do the same.

— Dr. Jack Martin; Burlington Biofuels Co-op;
Company Shops Food Co-op; Sustainable Development
program, Alamance Community College

To my brother Mark,
who has been my patron, my financial engineer,
and my friend for the past forty-five years.

Contents

Acknowledgments

In 1981 George McRobie published a book entitled *Small is Possible*. He was a colleague of E. F. Schumacher, the visionary economist who wrote *Small is Beautiful*, a term which was coined by his teacher, Leopold Kohr. McRobie's book is out of print, and reads like a catalogue of projects that have embodied Schumacher's wisdom.

I'm a fan of both Schumacher and McRobie. This book is coming from their tradition.

I need to acknowledge the people in this book. They are real. Their names are their names. And these stories about them are merely told by me. In *Sunshine Sketches of a Little Town*, Stephen Leacock pretends his characters are not real people. So does Mark Twain in *Life on the Mississippi*. I love both Leacock and Twain, and though some will surely claim this book belongs in the "fantasy" section of the bookstore, it's my take on the reality of our small town.

I should acknowledge Ingrid Witvoet at New Society. Before this was a book, it was an idea. I first bounced it off her in a snooty bar in Washington, DC after a long day at the Green Festival. Ideas need encouragement like hers to become manuscripts, and manuscripts take work, like hers, to become books.

I need to thank Julian Sereno, the publisher of the *Chatham County Line* for putting so much energy into keeping his newspaper afloat, and I would like to thank Mark Schultz, my editor at the *News and Observer*, who convinced me that community newspapers are the last bastions of independent thought. He once said, "If you can make energy sexy, you will be on to something."

I also need to thank the Fitzgerald family for lending me their house on Oak Island where I could work in peace. I am indebted to Pamela Bell and Jonathan Marvel for inviting us to their place at Southampton — a place where I could write and the children could run wild simultaneously. Jonathan served as a tour guide during our stay on Long Island, and in between nature expeditions, he illuminated the self reliant threads of that community. His insights into life in New York City, and summer in Southampton, have influenced the thinking in this book.

Stayce Leanza deserves some thanks for her creation of the map. She is an old roommate of mine at Moncure Chessworks and she is a fun inspiration to work with. And I need to thank McCayne Miller for helping me with software and for being so fun to talk with, and to look at. I also need to thank "The Women of Building One" for letting me hang out in their midst.

My own family needs acknowledgement for enduring the process of my writing these stories.

Sometimes I felt like one of the "primitives" in *Star Wars: The Phantom Menace*, who erect a bubble like force field around their army. My bubble for this book was at the kitchen table, keeping out Lego blocks and Playmobil figures. It isolated me from the movies, piano, and guitars playing in the next room. I am grateful to my wife Tami for her wisdom, which dictates that apart from the occasional smear of marmalade on the keyboard, our kitchen table is a fine place to write a book.

I would also like to acknowledge Tom McCarty. He passed through our town once, and like a current day Alexis de Tocqueville, published his observations online. Our biodiesel plant did not impress him. He'd seen much nicer operations. But he found our small town fascinating. He was intrigued by the sheer number of individuals running around on locally produced biodiesel, and by the vitality of Chatham Marketplace which was overflowing with locally produced food during his visit. His comments served as the genesis for this book.

And finally I would like to thank the readers of Energy Blog, who have commented, fed back, and encouraged me to keep telling stories about these characters.

Introduction

I once heard a story on National Public Radio about how delicious it is to eat a deep fried turkey, and I was intrigued. I started deep frying turkeys on special occasions and started wondering what to do with all of the left over fryer oil. I was exposed to biodiesel, and started using the waste vegetable oil to make fuel for my tractor.

The story of Piedmont Biofuels, which took Rachel, Leif and I from a barrel in the backyard to the corporate boardroom is chronicled in my first book, *Biodiesel Power: The Passion, the People and the Politics of the Next Renewable Fuel*. It ends just as we are about to embark on building a commercial biodiesel plant. By now we have finished that plant. We converted an abandoned industrial park on the edge of town into a thriving enterprise that manufactures and ships four thousand gallons of biodiesel a day.

By day I work at Piedmont Biofuels. As I was writing this book, I spent my days moving gallons of fuel into the world, and my nights moving words into this book.

But this is not the continuation of our story. Our story gets a chapter. While ours may well be an amazing project, it takes place inside the context of a dozen more.

Time changes every story inexorably. By the time *Biodiesel Power* came to market, everything had changed. When I referred to it as "obsolete," my editor at New Society, Ingrid, corrected my description to "a snapshot in time."

By the time this book arrives in bookstores, people will have fallen in love. And people will have moved away. And people will have died. And people will have traded in their partners for different models. Which means that this book too, is a snapshot.

In his book *The Great Turning*, David Korten lays out a vision based on five thousand years of human existence that states we are at a place where we can choose our destiny as a species. We can either continue on in our imperial ways on the road to ruining our garden planet, or we can begin "The Great Turning" toward a sustainable earth community. At the heart of Korten's thinking is the idea that we need to change our stories.

Unbeknownst to me, I was happily doing just that by publishing entries in Energy Blog. I was pushing out hundreds of vignettes — on everything from the visiting Fire Marshal to policy discussions to the time Rachel took a "golden shower" in used vegetable oil.

And remarkably it developed a following. Faraway readers came to identify with the real people in my life as if they were characters in a fictional tale.

This is non-fiction, folks.

This book gets some distance on biodiesel and takes forays into a broader world that is our small town.

I'm not an economist. But I have been wholly engaged in one sort of business or another in Chatham County for the past eighteen years, and for this book I have trolled those businesses (and others) for stories which might tell us something about how we can participate in the Great Turning of which Korten speaks.

I also think this book is partly an answer to some of the questions James Kunstler lays out in *The Long Emergency*. He is curious about whether or not we possess the vernacular knowledge to survive in the face of resource depletion and societal collapse, and in as much as this book is an investigation of his questions, the overwhelming answer is "yes, our community will be just fine."

PART I

Funky Town

Gotta make a move to a
Town that's right for me
Town to keep me movin'
Keep me groovin' with some energy

Lipps Inc., 1979

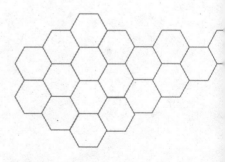

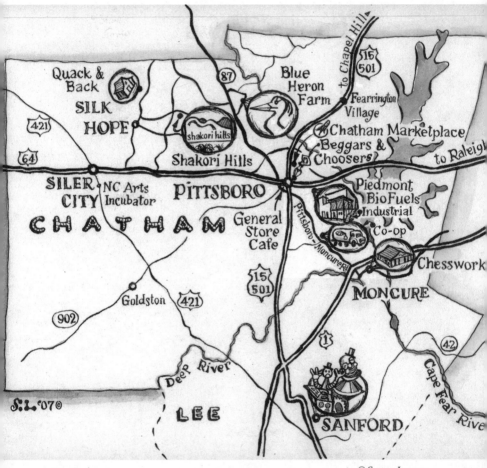

Silk Hope

LOCAL LEGEND has it that a wealthy merchant named Lutterloh once traveled to China and became enamored with silk worms. Apparently he loaded his ship with worms and plants and returned to Chatham County to found the community of Silk Hope, North Carolina.

Travelers through Silk Hope today find only an elementary school, an intersection with a gas station, and a small fairground run by the Ruritans, a civic service organization. Once a year they fire up their steam engine and host "Old Fashioned Farmer Days."

Silk, it would seem, was a bust. Perhaps the worms didn't care for the climate. Or perhaps our food soured their stomachs. Maybe the soils were wrong. Lutterloh remains a prosperous name, now known for a thriving trucking business that delivers crusher-run gravel to many of us when we repair our lanes, or make concrete from scratch.

And while silk may have been a bad idea in its day, there are vibrant signs of life in Silk Hope that are easy to miss on first pass. There is Celebrity Dairy, an astonishing bed-and-breakfast of considerable renown, which runs a herd of goats and a full-fledged dairy. In an era when North Carolina agriculture is flirting with "agri-tourism" as its next great hope, Celebrity Dairy is a pioneer. Brit and Fleming provide a resting spot to visitors to our county, and a place to host a wedding, but they also bring visitors from near and far when kidding time arrives.

It seems that every ounce of goat cheese is sold the moment it is produced, and for many the year is marked by those days when Celebrity Dairy products are in season. It arrives in co-op grocery stores, and on the menus of fancy restaurants as an early harbinger of spring.

Silk Hope is also home to the Body Therapy Institute, a pioneering massage school which has been graduating professional body workers for about as long as the profession has existed. From the road it is an unassuming place, but deep into the grounds it houses classrooms, dormitories, and parking lots filled with students. Many of which graduate, and stick around, leaving Chatham County with a disproportionately high masseuse-per-capita ratio.

Fran is a graduate. She lives one concession down with her husband John. Their children left the nest long ago, and they settled into immaculate country lives where she offers massage therapy up at the house, and he offers talk therapy down by the pond.

In many ways their neatly rowed gardens, and manicured orchard offer a counterbalance to those with frenetic lives. I doubt they have ever spent a penny on marketing their services, and I suspect their appointment books are full thanks to word of mouth.

My wife Tami and I have been going to John and Fran for years, and all indications are that we would like to continue to be their clients for as long as they stay in the therapy business. The fact that they do nothing to promote their services is anathema to us, as we are immersed in the go-go world of sales and marketing, and so we have invented an imaginary tag line for them that we refer to as "Quack and Back."

Every couple of weeks — or sometimes twice a week — or as schedules and budgets permit, we steal a morning and head to John and Fran's idyllic place in Silk Hope.

Tami always starts with a whole body massage up at the big house with Fran, while I pull up a chair across from John down at the "therapy shack." After an hour or so, we change places. I wrap up my session with the Quack, travel to the house, strip down and stretch out for an hour's worth of work on the Back.

It could be called marital therapy, although my ex-wife cannot stand the idea that both Tami and I see the same therapist. Or it could be considered simply a recess from our hectic lives. Tami spends her time on the massage table chatting with Fran, and I find myself asleep almost instantly.

When I am in dialog with John, I think of it more as a "practice," or as a time of study than as a time of therapy. He is a wiry, elfin looking fellow who exudes an inner calm. Put him in a robe and he would pass as a priest. Shave his head and he would pass as a Rinzai master. He appears utterly uninterested in station, however, and merely dons a t-shirt, ties back his ponytail, and walks through the woods to his off-grid therapy quarters to spend his days discussing reality with the likes of Tami and me.

John has a simple worldview that he espouses, and it is one that I have been trying to grasp. At its heart is the idea that we are often raised in a world that teaches scarcity. Because love is scarce, we must compete for affection. Because money is scarce, we must fight to accumulate as much as possible. Everything — from attention, to resources, to compliments — is in short supply, and so we are programmed from an early age to work to get our share.

His simple message is that such a world has it all wrong, and that in fact we live in a place of abundance, where the start point is that we get everything we want — or something better. He teaches that struggle is optional, and that we manifest our realities, and that we forge our lives exactly the way we want them.

I began exploring John's messages as a skeptic. Money was tight, my marriage to Tami was in trouble, business was tough, the kids were annoying, and I was locked in many pitched battles simultaneously.

As I began working with John, I timidly took a stab at some of his techniques, and to my amazement, found myself manifesting different results than those that I had normally known. The bank account began to fill up. Tami and I fell deeply in love. I mended some broken relationships with my children, and incredibly, found myself to be a believer.

I have never managed to find much spiritual traction. I don't care for ritual, and despite genuine efforts to immerse myself in Paganism, Methodism, Unitarian-Universalism, and Buddhism, I have never managed to find an abiding faith and have instead found myself feeding my soul from the bottom of the religious food chain.

Yet I have remained a student of John's. And as a result of my many years with him, I occasionally see a glimmer of mastery that I can call my own, and I have managed to manifest some interesting results.

In many ways, our remarkable journey into biodiesel, from a pole building behind my house which we call Summer Shop, to a multimillion dollar, many-faceted renewable energy conglomerate is the direct result of John's teachings.

On our advice, others in our circle have adopted the Quack and Back habit. And many others in our community were there before us — such that John's phrases are often quoted around town. It could be that Pittsboro is merely John's playground, in which he manifests a remarkable community that is capable of moving into abundance.

My daughter Kaitlin rejects John's teachings, and fails to see why anyone would go back to see him month after month. She feels that "the something even better" is a trap that keeps me going back for more and is merely a ploy by John to take my money into his retirement.

At age 15, Kaitlin's point of view is refreshing — and she offers wisdom on virtually every aspect of our lives. If Tami and I are merely a living 401K for John and Fran, we are happy to play the role.

And the reason to return over and over again is that it is hard to overcome old programming. Sometimes I manage to practice John's teaching, and when I do I find myself manifesting remarkable results. And sometimes I slip back into the ways of old, in which I choose struggle and see the world through the lens of scarcity rather than abundance.

I figure going to church is the same way. The essential messages are easy to grasp: Christ died for my sins, or my mind is a jumping monkey, or the planet is our mother. Most people can get their heads around the tenets of religion quickly and easily, but the reason to return week after week is because without the reminder, or "top up" so to speak, the easy to grasp tenets are quickly forgotten.

John's practice is one approach that I follow. Through the filter of his philosophy it is entirely possible to measure Silk Hope not by the absence of silk worms, but rather by the presence of so many thriving business endeavors.

When I take the Silk Hope road to John's, the fecundity starts at Gum Springs Garage, where Roy continually chomps on a half smoked Tampa Sweet, and where mechanics gather around the woodstove. They can fix anything — all in good time — and it would be by stopping in, not by telephone that most updates on work are passed along.

I then pass Louis' place, where they run a small sawmill, and make cedar chests, and coat hangers, and where they run a small cow-calf operation, along with vegetable production. You can see multiple generations about the place, from young children weeding vast beds of broccoli to Louis' father loading up a trailer of rough-cut wood.

It's a hopeful road, on the way to Quack and Back, despite the failure of silk.

My brother Jim shares some overlapping philosophy with John. He is an insatiable entrepreneur who insists he be measured not by the vast pile of bad ideas, heaped at the bottom of the wall — but rather by those ideas that stuck. As a risk-taker he has figured out a way to stay in the possible, and not dwell on those ventures that stung him.

At Piedmont Biofuels, many of us have internalized the teachings of John, and we have distilled it down to an expression that we call "staying in the Ray."

Ray is a resident of Blue Heron farm, the co-housing community down Lutterloh Road just past Gums Springs Garage. One day when Rachel and I were working the booth at the Shakori Grassroots Festival of Music and Dance, Ray approached our table. We chatted idly about one thing and another, and when he realized he was in the presence of Rachel, he lit up brightly.

"You're Rachel Burton?" he said. "Thank you. Thank you for teaching down at the college, and for being a female mechanic, for setting an example for my daughters, for being so generous with your knowledge. Thank you so much for all you do."

Rachel was taken aback. And beaming.

That night she collided with some struggle in her personal life, and we talked on the phone. I asked her if she remembered her encounter with Ray earlier in the day. Of course she did. And I wondered if she could set down her troubles of that moment and think back to when Ray was showering her with gratitude.

"Stay in the Ray," I said, and we have all attempted to get back to that moment many, many times along the way.

Whether it comes from a therapy session with John, or from the optimism of my brother Jim, or from a chance encounter with Ray, the message is the same. Anything's possible, we can manifest any reality we desire. We might not make a lot of silk in these parts, but there is certainly no lack of hope.

Global Producers

I HAVEN'T ALWAYS been enmeshed in the local economy. Quite the opposite. For many years I bought into the "you must be global to survive" concept. And I took the global economy bait, hook, line, and sinker.

I was stopped at the light by The Manor when I heard the newscast on the CBC. The Manor was a strip club in an old stone turreted building that I passed on my way to and from work. Researchers had identified a new medical syndrome they were calling Seasonal Affective Disorder. I peered through the sloshing windshield wipers at the grey sky and realized I had suffered from it all of my life. They had a given a name to the winter blues. The marquis at the Manor said that Sugar and Spice were in town. And I promised myself that it was time to permanently move to a sunny, warm, faraway place.

At the time I was in my brother's technology business. I was a traveling salesman responsible for distant markets. We were head quartered in Guelph, Ontario, and I spent most of my days in Vancouver, or Winnipeg, or Halifax. For a time it felt as if I awoke in Guelph and commuted to Montreal.

The alleged cure for Seasonal Affective Disorder was to spend some time beneath bright lights. It sounded crackpot to me. In my view we had a bright light, it was the sun, and all I had to do was move to a part of the world where there was more of it. My brothers indicated it would be fine for me to move to the United States, as long as we were fully engaged in every large market opportunity in Canada.

Canada is a big place. In order to get us positioned in all Canadian markets I opened branch offices. And I lived on airplanes. When I finally managed to move to the south I left behind enough frequent flyer points to go to Hong Kong and back. For two.

I moved to the United States in search of blue sky and sunshine, to follow the shifting technology markets which were feeling the sharp elbow of the newly enacted North American Free Trade Act (NAFTA). In one sense I was our emissary to the global economy — sent from afar to internationalize the family business.

Since I merely set out to create a living for one, I had my choice of all the sunshiny markets America had to offer. California was expensive. And at the time it was suffering from drought. Texas would have been a good choice, but moving from Canada to the United States was enough culture shock, and I was afraid I could not handle moving to Texas, which appeared to be its own separate country. So I settled on the Research Triangle Park (RTP) of North Carolina, where things were cheap, and there was plenty of water and a growing technology market.

There was a time when I would start each day at my new home in the woods before first light. I would put on my coat and tie and head to my office on the edge of RTP. It was a long drive on a two-lane road, and there was a good chance of getting stuck behind a tractor pulling a load of tobacco or cotton during the harvest times. I spent my days running from the boardroom to the plant floor, and from factories to retailers, selling technology from Canada.

I would return home each night after dark, to my wood-stove, and my outhouse, and to a rickety kitchen table full of friends who liked to sit around and talk about forming "community." We read books by Scott Peck, and went to weekend conferences with the likes of Thomas Berry, and we speculated long into many nights about theoretical constructs on how humans might better live together.

Each morning I would leave the woods and rush back to my little enterprise, where I would import goods from Japan, and flip them into Montreal. I would bring down a load from Ontario, and distribute it all over the United States. I was an entrepreneur with my toe in the global economy. I read books on time management, and I read Tom Peters, who promised everyone that if we didn't have a percentage of our businesses in the international markets, we were certainly doomed.

To this day the brothers in my family hold different opinions. My brother Jim, who started the company, is now a technology mogul with business tentacles all over the globe. He likes to jokingly describe me as a nepotistic charity case that was writing poetry prior to getting a real job with his company. I like to assure him that my tireless effort made him the man he is today.

We all were captains of industry, with big plans and big deals, which is why I was surprised when I overheard my father refer to the collective effort of his sons as a "little computer sales and service company." We were conquering the world, yet he described us as if we were a local lawnmower shop.

He spent his career in the manufacture and distribution of control valves for customers around the planet. Part of his task was to right size the factories to the markets. And to keep the unions happy. Part of his success came from figuring out how to think like a Canadian. As an immigrant to Canada, he aced that part, and he subsequently delivered the Canadian market to his global masters.

We grew up with visitors at the dining room table, from Mexico, and South Africa, and from parts unknown. As children we had a grasp of McLuhan's "global village," even though the highlight of our week was the family trip to our local farmer's market.

When I immigrated to the United States, I was intent on delivering profits back to our Canadian headquarters. I was taught to check my anti-business bias in favor of black ink.

My brother Mark, a former union organizer, also managed to reconcile his management-labor beliefs in the name of the family business, and he eventually joined me in our international efforts.

Tami jumped into the game and joined us with relish. She would land a deal in Turkey, and fulfill it from Canada, and she would fly to California on the promise of more leads.

It wasn't long before Tami and I became an item, and when she joined me in the woods of Chatham County, she was suspicious of ecovillages and co-counseling and all such talk of radical changes to the way people should live.

And while she kept her distance from the long, complex arguments that were ongoing at the kitchen table, her presence didn't change our love for theoretical conversations about "community." While activists and organizers talked late into the night, the unincorporated village of Moncure, where we lived, was in the throes of a bruising battle over whether or not it should become a town. We were oblivious to the actual life in our community. We missed the meetings in the fire hall, and missed the petition drives at Ray's Supermarket.

We were newcomers, and outsiders who simply lived here. Our concept of community was abstract. Instead of putting our names on a petition, we were reading books about societal change. Instead of voting, were debating the concept of democracy.

While we explored structures that would permit us to vote for the inclusion of prospective neighbors, our actual neighbors were actively involved in the life of the community. In our make-believe world, different people assumed different tasks. Some worked on the farm to produce food. Some worked at micro-enterprise to produce products we would need.

The process and the people intrigued me, and I loved the fantasy. I think everyone assumed that I would simply be the person responsible for "cash inputs" since I spent far too much time in airports to be actively engaged in the creation of community.

I was wedded to the global economy. My outpost of the family business had grown substantially, and I found myself traveling the globe to do deals on behalf of our vendors. I spent considerable time in the "Technology from Canada" booths in Germany, and Las Vegas, and Budapest. I found myself at parties in embassies, and consulates around the world, and with my selling skills in high demand; I was routinely flown to Caribbean countries for conversations on how to close the next big deal.

Mine is not a John Perkins story. He's the author of *Confessions of an Economic Hit Man* who knowingly checked his conscience in exchange for riches. I thought I was on the right path. I worked in concert with my brothers, on a quest for a billion dollar empire. I genuinely didn't know any better.

I was running a profitable, ethical corporation. I was creating jobs. I was generating wealth. I stabbed no one in the back, saw no need to crush anyone below me, and if business is to be described as a "dog eat dog" activity, I had no occasion to "eat dog."

My employees tended to stay with me for many years; I won awards for workplace culture, for family friendly environments, and for waste reduction. I had a disciplined program of charitable giving, and donated a percentage of my profits to local charities in the markets where the profits were produced. We all did. The family business was simply a good thing.

I gave money to our local National Public Radio affiliate, and to Family Violence and Rape Crisis, and to the Carnivore Preservation Trust, and to the Chatham Arts Council, and to the Education Foundation, and to a host of other local causes that I believed in. My company's name was on the rolls of pretty much every charity in Chatham County.

On one of the rare occasions when I was in town long enough to participate in civic life, I went to a town hall meeting only to hear one of my activist buddies proclaim that it was "transnational corporations that are the problem."

I was a transnational. I didn't see a problem, exactly. In the ancient world Hermes was the god of travel. He's the fellow with the wings on his boots. It was business people who tended to be the travelers, so Hermes was the god of business. Thieves also traveled. So Hermes was the god of thieves. I spent a couple of decades traveling on business, and never had to participate in the thieving part.

Although I did have a sense that something was wrong.

I saw the pure wastage of international business. And I started worrying about life on the planet. In an effort to remember my days as a "global producer," I delved back into my journal entries. Before pouring my heart out on Energy Blog, I used to journal occasionally, and I found an entry that was penned in a sidewalk café on Avenida Libarado in Lisbon, Portugal on May

8, 1995. I had just paid sixty thousand escudos for a night in a hotel, and I reflected:

> As I walk past restaurants and prostitutes and night clubs familiar from the prior evenings, it occurs to me that in my four days here I have spent close to two thousand US dollars, or roughly twenty percent of the average Portuguese wage earner's yearly take.
>
> Pondering the energy required to come by two thousand dollars is a daunting task. With an equal sum I could spare one thousand hectares of Amazon rainforest. Or I could adopt a kinkajou in Pittsboro and provide it with sustenance and habitat for three years. Two thousand dollars is more than a Cabloco family will spend in a generation, and yet, it's been a delightful four days in Lisbon.

It was starting to dawn on me that I did more environmental destruction with my commuting than several generations of Cabloco farmers in the Amazon. I once canoed a portion of the Amazon and I saw multiple families sharing a single machete. At the time it was fashionable to knock Brazil for the "burning of the rainforest," and traveling through the fires made me wonder about my own business travel.

Waste worried me. When I left my home and native land, the City of Guelph was ticketing people at the curb for failure to properly sort their recyclables. When I arrived in Raleigh, North Carolina, they were still tossing everything into the landfill. There was no recycling. I'm not sure I even was an environmentalist at the time. But when you're in the recycling habit, it's hard to throw an aluminum can in the trash.

I had an ingrained sense that the failure to recycle items into new products was wrong-headed. When I was in high school in the late seventies, my father and I would tote tin cans down to ARC Industries to be resold into the metal markets. He grew up in the Depression, and wasted virtually nothing.

Moving to a culture that had no sense of recycling jarred me. It awoke the desire for change. When I decided to use recycled cardboard boxes for our shipments, we gobbled up all of the cardboard of two neighboring office buildings. I started shredding fine paper for use as packaging materials, and I pushed several vendors on design changes for their product packaging. We implemented a "buy green" purchasing policy back in the late 1980s.

We were "greening" our operation before the term had been invented. And we weren't doing it to gain market share. We were doing it because it felt like the right thing to do.

Although we were not running foundries, or locomotives, we were producing. We were kicking out a lot of wealth. Ayn Rand would have been impressed. Our names appeared on a bunch of donor lists. And we employed a lot of people.

We were simply utilizing our skills to exploit markets and opportunities that happened to be global in nature. There was a nagging sense that something was wrong with the trajectory of our lives, as we shuttled back and forth from the airport to our piece of paradise in the woods, but we were not sure what that something was.

We were deep in what David Korten refers to as the "Imperial Consciousness." We were building an empire.

⬡⬡⬡

There was a time when "casual Fridays" meant less starch in our button-down collars. We used to sit around our lunchroom table, in our coats and our ties, discussing the new trend in corporate apparel that we had heard about.

We mused about the local economy, and speculated about our role within it, but we were so immersed in our corporate endeavors, it was a mere topic of conversation — sort of like new trends in office apparel.

That was until I bought BLAST, and moved it to Pittsboro.

Before it came to Pittsboro, BLAST was a slick little communications tool that Dan and Polly Henderson and their company had developed in Baton Rouge. It would be nice to say it came from the swamps of Louisiana, but a more accurate description would be to say that it came from the petrochemical soup and smog that is Baton Rouge.

BLAST was an acronym for Blocked Asynchronous Transmission, which was a sliding-window protocol that was exceedingly helpful for moving files around — especially well-suited for noisy phone lines.

Dan and Polly had created a remarkable software company.

Their little business suited our burgeoning distribution efforts perfectly. They shoveled out the new features, we sold their software all over Canada and the United States, and they helped us every way they could. This was the time of the nascent Internet, which meant we were also selling modems at an amazing clip. The tired cliché from the business literature of the day was about the Internet gold rush, in which we were the ones selling shovels and pans.

Then US Robotics purchased BLAST, and crushed it, and we were all taken for a bruising ride through the public markets. They were an up and coming manufacturer of industrial modems who had an eye on conquering the world. Stock market analysts told them that before they could go public, they needed to be both a hardware and a software vendor, and so they plucked BLAST out of Louisiana, moved it to Skokie, Illinois and positioned it as window dressing for what would become one of the most spectacular stock offerings in history.

Their clunky modems were replaced by a consumer product which they produced every minute and a half. They went on to see their names on the *Fortune* magazine list of wealthy individuals, and BLAST was forgotten like the child's toy that breaks on Christmas morning.

We took the punishment from an install base of loyal customers who had been abandoned.

When we called US Robotics for bug fixes, they informed us that product had been discontinued. When we made a sale that was significant for us, they informed us they could no longer manufacture for that platform. And when the loyal BLAST users called for relief, all we could offer was consolation instead of new revisions.

I used to sit around the office after hours with our core staff, and we would frequently migrate toward a speculative conversation on "What would you do if you owned BLAST?"

"I'd pick up the phone when it rang," said one.

"I'd call people back when they left messages," said another.

"I think I'd develop a product for Windows," said another.

I would leave these conversations, and return to my shack, where I would warm water on the woodstove for a shave, and rejoin the constant prattle of grants and fellowships and gardens that were largely imaginary in nature.

We all knew that BLAST was on its way to extinction, and we mourned the opportunity that we knew would be lost.

I distinctly remember the morning when I was walking to my Honda Accord to begin my usual massive commute, when I was overtaken by a moment of clarity. This was before I had started practicing with John, yet it was a study in manifestation.

It struck me in one moment that I actually *could* buy the company.

Which is what I did. I met my brothers in Skokie, we did the negotiations, US Robotics shuttled me around in a limousine, and within months we had a deal.

It was the eve of my first acquisition, and it was a heady time. I needed a place to locate the new company, and I needed staff to run it. Instead of inking some space in the go-go action of Research Triangle Park, I decided to gamble on putting the project in Pittsboro. It was a sleepy little farm town five miles from my house, and one of its many abandoned spaces was a bankrupt Mediterranean restaurant that was about the right size.

Industry pundits advised me that I would not be able to attract the necessary talent in a place like Pittsboro, and that I needed to locate closer to the action. I wondered about that. I thought that perhaps the woods of Chatham County was full of talent that was doing the same thing I was — which was hustling around the Park all day and returning to the "paradise" which we seldom had time to enjoy.

The only thing I knew about Pittsboro was that it was close. I turned to my friend Barbara Lorie for guidance and advice, and she took time off from the formation of her cohousing community to help me out.

She pointed me to Sandy, the Zen priest who did renovation work, and he transformed the Mediterranean restaurant into office space. The space was barely ready when the deal closed and two eighteen-wheelers embarked from Skokie for Pittsboro.

The manager of the Town of Pittsboro did not know how to grant a business license to a software company. He was a creative and flexible man, and after enough conversation we concurred that it would probably be okay if we were permitted to open under the category of "Small Appliance Repair."

When the trucks arrived they blocked traffic in front of the Post Office, and I went on a hiring spree. I had space which was almost completed — we left the Mediterranean palm trees painted on the wall — I had truckloads of computers and source code and boxes of product, and I had phones that were ringing with the fifteen-year-old vanity phone number that I had insisted be included with the deal.

What I needed was staff. My sales manager, Steve, left my side in RTP and took up with BLAST. As did Tami. As did my brother Mark, who parachuted in from Canada. But I needed more help than that. Barbara patiently directed me to all available talent.

There was Doug, who was writing a chemistry textbook. He abandoned his academic pursuits and joined BLAST to write documentation. After all, writing is writing. There was Sam, who was running a snack truck. Shipping is shipping, after all. Snacks, software — just ship it out on time.

Leon ran the furniture store around the corner. His passion was for elaborate wooden models of transport trucks and fire engines, and he was a remarkable craftsman. I'm not sure how healthy the furniture market in Pittsboro was at the time, but he had hand trucks, and he had a son, Brian, who had a strong back and a good attitude toward work. Brian unloaded our eighteen-wheelers — as his civic duty to help clear traffic congestion — and hired on to work in technical support. Brian worked with us for over a decade before realizing his dream of becoming one of the first professional fire fighters hired by Chatham County.

Barbara found Barbara, a local accountant, who was frustrated by her endeavors for a local CPA and who was delighted to become the Chief Financial Officer of BLAST.

We were in business over night. The phones were ringing, and we were shipping product all over the planet from the heart of downtown Pittsboro. We joked that we didn't need to lock our doors at night, since we only possessed a million dollars worth of computer gear. Had we been selling farm equipment, we would have needed a fence.

BLAST was a truly global business. It had distributors on every continent, and product installed in almost every country on earth. Faxes rolled in with orders from far away places, and BLAST delivered.

I was still donning a coat and tie and vanishing into my monster commute to RTP and the family business, when Tami started going to work in her blue jeans. She did need to pick up her dry cleaning before her trips to Paris, or Milan, or Mexico City, but she found her Pittsboro days could be spent in her casual clothes.

"None of our customers come to Pittsboro," she said. "They'll never see us dressed this way."

In no time the company lost its business attire, at which point I was instantly jealous.

I watched my colleagues moving on to more meaningful employment, where they could wear what they wanted to wear, and be who they wanted to be. With leftover palm trees on the wall, an expansive deck out back, and a ping-pong table in the basement, they went to work on shipping product.

Tami and I shared a humble farmhouse in the woods, which somehow got electricity and running water shortly after her arrival, but our conduit for communication was through Lisa, our travel agent.

Lisa would say, "You are going to be in Portland, and Tami is going to be in San Francisco for the weekend — would you like me to get you together?" Although Tami had left the family business in favor of small town software, she was still very much on the global stage.

At is peak, BLAST was running a nineteen person payroll, including Dennis Kikendall and Will Raymond, arguably the greatest minds in communication software in the area. We successfully shifted the trajectory of its descent into the Dumpster, and along the way we buried all of its corporate debt, and assembled a pile of cash. My gamble that there would be plenty of talent in the woods paid off handsomely. Many people were delighted to forgo higher salaries to work closer to home.

We had a blast at BLAST. And it introduced us to Pittsboro, North Carolina, the community on the other end of the Pittsboro-Moncure Rd. upon which we live. Many of the hours I spent working for BLAST was in far away lands, on the floor of a trade show, or sharing exotic meals with distributors. I would pass through town on my way to and from work — always over dressed — but I was finally getting a chance to see things in the light of day.

I opened an account at the local hardware store — to buy the odds and ends necessary to maintain the business. Donnie and Joyce ran the place, and whenever I walked into the store in the early days, I did not look like the other patrons. Nonetheless, they came to accept me over time, and I found myself drawn to their wisdom and advice.

I opened a bank account on the corner, at a place that has never been able to comprehend foreign currency exchange. I moved all of my travel to the local travel agency two doors down from the bank. My introduction to Pittsboro was that of an absentee property owner, occasionally stopping by for meetings or to run errands on behalf of the property. With BLAST, we shifted from absentee members of the community, to identifiable merchants in its midst.

I occasionally went to lunch about town, and sometimes stopped in at Mimi's General Store. She was selling a slim selection of organic vegetables and a whole bunch of health food supplements. Mimi and I became friends. She had been retailing in Pittsboro for many years, and I was the new guy with a software company.

On one occasion we were sitting on the front porch of my ramshackle home and Mimi was discussing a bold move. She was contemplating moving out of the ground floor of the Blair Hotel and into the abandoned car dealership next to the courthouse. More importantly, she was thinking about serving lunch.

I told her that the highly paid people of BLAST would pay a premium for organic lunches, and that the demographic shift in Pittsboro was under way.

Along the way we had befriended Clyde Jones, a legendary "outsider artist" who cuts "critters" out of cedar logs with his chain saw. We provided Clyde with rides, and cedar logs from our place, and he occasionally gave us a sculpture that he usually made on site.

One time I helped Clyde negotiate a royalty deal with the New Orleans Museum of Art. Clyde sat on one side of the kitchen table and listened to my phone conversation. I attempted to represent his best interests on my side of the table — taking visual cues from him. When we finished the deal, they emailed me a form to be signed, and I suggested to Clyde that we get him a copy for his records. To do that, we dropped in at BLAST.

At the time BLAST was right next door to the Post Office, and it boasted a long brick wall. As Clyde and I were entering the building, I suggested the wall was ugly, to which he agreed. We decided on a whim that if I were to get the wall painted blue, and provide some scaffolding, he would paint a mural on it.

Which we did. Tami rounded up school children, the local hardware store's paint vendor donated the paint, and off we went.

The mural went up in fine fashion. Someone called the police, thinking it was a violation of the local sign ordinance, but when the chief of police came to inspect, he thought it looked fine to him.

I miscalculated the amount of media attention the project would receive. It seemed like every camera crew and newspaper in the state arrived to cover the famous Clyde Jones doing a mural, and BLAST failed to get a single mention.

Later I heard through the small town grapevine that the project had been self-serving, since it made such a big media splash. Before the project I had very little experience with the local media, so I learned from the rumor, and thought, "That was just a big ugly wall — if you want self serving, I'll show you self serving..."

We tried to capitalize on the event by publishing a "Greetings from Pittsboro" postcard, which we used for correspondence with customers all over the world, but at the end of the day the mural was an object lesson in how not to garner publicity for ourselves.

Today the muralized building is one part government office, and one part hairdressing salon. Both of my sons got Mohawk haircuts there last summer. The Post Office has moved to the edge of town and its old residence is abandoned.

BLAST's future was wiped out by the Internet, and as a property it is remembered fondly by Information Technology folks everywhere. Tami left to have babies, Mark and I were swept away by our growing distribution enterprise, and those who were left behind never figured out how to retool the company for the current day.

Something I learned along the way is that all business is difficult. One moment you are distributing computer memory in Canada, and you find that you are operating on razor thin margins and that the business is tough. Since you naturally want to be in an "easier" business, you look around at customers and suppliers to see who has it easy.

In the computer business the vendors with the highest margins are in software. It costs them a dollar to print a compact disc worth of software, and they sell it for sixteen hundred bucks. BLAST was my foray into software. What is not included in the compact disc printing cost is the million dollars worth of research and development that goes in to produce un-saleable products that do not go to market. And we did a lot of that at BLAST. We would work for years on products that would miss the market entirely. It turned out that being in the software business was hard.

And I think the same lesson applies to biodiesel. On the surface it is the process of taking waste fat, oil, and grease and converting them to fuel. Easy money. It's a business where you can sell every drop you produce without trying.

Except it appears to be exceptionally difficult to make any money doing it.

Which has left me with the conclusion that all business is hard.

Which is the opposite message from what John would tell me. And both messages are correct. Business is hard. It takes work. And when you are in business you get everything you want or something better from your endeavors.

I should note that earnings are not the only yardstick I have used to measure whether or not something is a success. Once when Tami and I were riding horseback to the lost Jordanian city of Petra, I was not reflecting on how much money had been lost or wasted along the way.

Rather, I was vigorously celebrating the global economy that had been so kind to us.

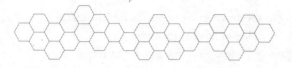

Going to Town

There's a metal sculptor in Rockwood, Ontario named Andreas Drenters. He worked with his brother to assemble a remarkable sculpture called Pioneer Family. It was a larger-than-life Conestoga wagon, complete with children and dogs that made its debut in Montreal at Expo 67.

I remember Expo 67. When we went as a family I was five years old. We believed in World Fairs.

And I later became friends with Andreas. He worked out of a tiny shop in Rockwood, Ontario, and filled the grounds of an abandoned nunnery with magnificent pieces of scrap metal sculpture. He was an inspiration to me.

When I bought my farm in Moncure, it was covered with trash. In a time before landfills, tradition dictated that you tote your garbage to the property line and form a pile. When your neighbor did the same thing, everything was clear. Which means the busted subsistence farms which dot these woods are demarcated by trash. While some has decomposed over the years, the metal remains.

I came along in the era of public landfills, but the instinctive recycler in me would not let me throw metal away.

I sorted glass by color. And I bagged aluminum cans by the ton. And whenever I could, I would load my pickup truck up with ferrous metals, and drive to Siler City, where I would sell it to John over at Bish Enterprises. Bish is a scrap yard and army surplus store. John would pay around a penny a pound, which meant a good day would result in five bucks. On my way home empty, I would stop at the stockyard, and give my money to the fellow who mucked out the stalls with the Bobcat.

He was supposed to load people for free on certain afternoons, but he got accustomed to my scrap-metal tip and was happy to hook me up with a scoop or two of fresh manure. My poor old truck would ride low with a load of metal to Siler City, and return riding low with soil amendment.

I would occasionally do the trip with my daughters, in which each of us would guess the weight of the outgoing load. The winner would pocket the money, which generally meant we came home with milkshakes instead of manure.

But after years of hauling from the woods to the scrap yard, I started seeing things in the metal. I would fish out certain pieces, drill holes in them with my electric drill, and bolt them together. Tami would come home from work, and I would say "Look, honey, there's a mosquito in the front yard."

She would look at the "sculpture," which had tin cans for eyes, and she would look at me with a worried expression. Using a hand-held hacksaw, and nuts and bolts, I made caterpillars, and a giant Canada goose, and flowers for the yard.

Friends and family started noticing when they came to visit, and they occasionally asked to purchase a piece. "Mother's day is coming up, and my Mom would like that," Phifer said. At the time I was running around Research Triangle Park each day trying to sell software for a living, and I had no desire to sell my art. Which made me politely decline.

That only increased demand.

My journey into art was triggered in large part by a trip to Sweden. Tami and I awoke one morning in Hanover, Germany, at the end of a grueling technology trade show, and boarded a train for Sweden.

It was Easter, and though Sweden is not a religious country, the place was largely closed. The service was horrible, the weather was drab, and my fantasies about Sweden as the model progressive country were abruptly dashed. On top of my broken expectations, Tami and I decided that it would probably be best if we split the sheets on our return.

She wanted kids. I already had kids. And we pretty much agreed that it would be best if we went our separate ways.

We were in Uppsala, visiting a church renowned for its Viking runes, and as we walked through the cold drizzle, thoroughly disheartened, we encountered a garden-sized chess set made of wood set in a private glen in a public park.

It was a miraculous affair. We played a game. It was fun.

I thought of my scrap metal piles at home, and envisioned a life-sized set made from scrap. For some reason, it occurred to me that if we could have a giant-sized chess set at home, having more children with Tami wouldn't be that bad.

I built my big board, and Zafer arrived, and our love of corporate life evaporated.

Tami went back to work for one week, cried her eyes out, and traded in her jet-set job for motherhood. She decided to become an art broker, which she intended to do with a kid on her hip, from her headquarters in the corner of our living room. And she kicked off her new business by selling a life-sized chess set to Laura over at Reba and Roses, which was a renowned landscaping and garden art center.

With an "order" in hand, I needed to get busy, and I quickly realized that I had no way to do real welding. I collected all the design elements for the first set, and had them welded together by John Amero over at Amero Metal Design. He gave me a lesson in how to operate my oxy-fuel rig, and then left me to my own devices.

I landed a one-man exhibition at the Carrboro Art Center, called Junkyard Frog, for which I braised my brains out.

I collected some interesting scrap metal from an abandoned mill and made a piece which I called "Going to Town." It was a family on a buckboard. Mom, Dad, daughter, son, dog, pulled by horse. When braising cast iron the trick is to use nickel rods and to sand-cool the joints. I put a tractor tire in place at Summer Shop, and filled it with sand. I would complete a joint, and immerse it in the sand, let it cool, and pull it out for the next one. And I did this a hundred times to fabricate Going to Town.

When Going to Town showed up in the Carrboro Arts Center, I paid tribute to Andreas Drenters and Pioneer Family. Its scale was tiny compared to his. But his influence was evident. The show was selected as one of the top ten exhibitions in the Triangle for 1998.

It wasn't long before I realized that if I was going to make a go of metal sculpture, I would need to be indoors, and I would need better electricity, and I would need to learn how to actually weld.

That combination of ideas put me on the real estate hunt. Anyone headed out of our house has a twisted half-mile drive to the end of the lane. When they reach the Pittsboro-Moncure Road upon which we live, they will find themselves about equidistant between the two places. Take a left and you are headed for Moncure. Take a right and you are Pittsboro bound.

The day I decided to search for a place to set up shop I took a left.

The unincorporated village of Moncure has a handful of churches, a post office, the Jordan Dam Mini Mart, an elementary school, a bank, a post office, and Ray's General Merchandise — which is a Citgo station with a butcher shop and about anything else someone might need.

My desire was to not only open a sculpture business, but also to open an "arts incubator," where other artists would rent space, come into their own, and settle in Moncure. I saw the Village of Moncure as the next Soho. Real Estate was cheap, places were abandoned, and I figured it would be easy to effect an "artistic renaissance" in the community.

The site I chose was a single story white building on Old US 1, about the middle of town. Elbert had won it in a poker game, and his wife Claudia ran a beauty salon in one of its rooms.

I needed some cash to launch the project, so I headed down into the hollow where Wilbur and Margaret lived. Margaret was a county commissioner at the time, and was an emissary from the black community. Her brother Wilbur is our county's greatest salesman. Whether it is pumpkins, or firewood, or collard greens, or whatever, he has been selling products off the back of his truck for generations, and is undoubtedly one of the wealthiest individuals in Moncure.

I explained my vision to them. They were to donate money to the Botanical Garden in Chapel Hill, and the Botanical Garden was to buy one of my giant chess sets. I was to take the money, and transform Elbert and Claudia's place into Moncure Chessworks, which would then incubate studio artists, introduce the community to chess, teach chess to children, and otherwise transform the community.

They liked the idea. And they were in.

With an order in hand, I rented the place and went to work. A dear friend from college, Jim, jumped in and helped with the transformation of the building.

We moved in together as artistic roommates, intent on making our way as studio artists.

The building had enjoyed a long and varied life, but the most famous of its incarnations was that of juke joint. In a village where there was no such thing as liquor by the drink, Elbert managed to create a thriving speak easy, with live bands, a VIP lounge, and a reputation which drew black folks from miles around.

We turned the stage into a spray booth, rigged up compressed air, and I set up a metal working shop where the VIP room once stood.

I hosted chess tournaments, at one point bringing in Emory Tate, who at the time was slotted to become the first African American grand master chess player. I offered chess lessons. And with the help of the masonry class from Northwood High School, I built a twenty-four square foot solid concrete chess board in the side yard.

As the years wore on Elsie painted a mural on the side wall, and Mike built an outdoor grinding station and scrap yard. Jim moved a kiln in, and we started having openings that would draw a crowd. Kerry moved into one corner and worked in stained glass. The place began to pulse, and whenever I landed big commissions, whether they were chess sets, or otherwise, I would take on help. Stayce and Stacey and Heather and Janice and I had a blast shipping everything from giant toys, to giant steel teacups, to thematic chess sets.

By far the greatest transformation came from Jim Massey who lived down the road at the Holly Hill Daylily farm. He was the first person to ever "buy" a sculpture from me. Jim is a connoisseur of botanical life, and a purveyor of registered, named, and hybridized daylilies, among other things.

His artistic sensibility is unique, and he has become an avid collector of "outsider and visionary" art. Back then he would simply take a pair of manikin legs, dress them in ruby slippers, wedge them beneath his newly constructed gazebo, and refer to the piece as "Dorothy."

He's built gardens around his headless Madonna collection, and constructed a giant mound of hollyhocks "because nobody ever features them, you know."

The Holly Hill Daylily Farm is an ever-changing place that is full of surprises with each visit, and more importantly, full of Jim. He brims with stories, and sentiments and advice, and loves to poke fun at the establishment, all the while bemoaning how hard it is to stay in business. After each season I ask him how his year went, and each year is "Awful, just awful — thirty percent less than last year." Despite that, his farm has rapidly expanded. New buildings, and ponds, and sculpture — it is a remarkable place.

On the occasion of my first sale, I drove to his place in the rain. I had fashioned a clump of daylilies out of steel strapping and some bicycle parts. I left the sculpture on the truck, slipped through his gate and walked up to his house.

He came to the door cautiously. I explained that I had been making scrap metal sculptures, and that I had never sold one, and that I had made one which I thought he would like, and that I would be happy to install it for him under one condition.

"That is, if you like it, you have to buy it."

He thought that was a reasonable proposition, and so he sent me, and one of his minions down to the front field to do the install. As we were finishing, he came lumbering down from the house, beneath a full sized patio umbrella that was being carried by another of his associates.

As he approached, he said to his first assistant, "Will I like it?"

The answer came back, "Oh, yes."

He stepped up and studied the sculpture and immediately turned to me (who was soaking wet by this time) and said, "I'll take it. How much?"

It was my moment of truth. I was professional salesman. And I caved. I had no idea.

I said, "I don't know. I could take flowers. Whenever I come shopping here, I dig from this side of the path," pointing to the area where the plants tended to be in the seven to ten dollar range. "If you would like, you could pay with plants from that side," pointing to the area where the new releases were growing. Newly released plants could be twenty-five to a hundred and fifty dollars each, and while I always marveled at them, I could not afford them.

"All right" he said, motioning to one off his workers, let's give him a Holly Hill Sunset, and dig a couple of Festival Enos, and here, get him some…" and he sent me home with over three hundred and fifty dollars worth of plants.

I had sold my first sculpture. And I had gone from a gardener to a "collector of daylilies." It was unbelievable.

When Chessworks came to town, Jim remained suspicious. He would stop by occasionally and tell stories and chat, and he kept abreast of the new work. But he was not a buyer in the early days.

Once he had me weld a child's bicycle into a wheelie for a display he was working on, which I believe I did for free. And eventually he would pick up the odd piece here and there. When I had help, he would happily pay them to grind out posts or install art fencing for him. His own deer fence, which he has been

building out of bicycles for about a decade, may yet prove too
labor intensive to complete.

A turning point for Chessworks was an occasion when
Jim indicated that if I would put a planter out in my full sun,
cracked asphalt parking lot; he would fill it with plants. I ignored the idea until one day when I was at the scrap yard with
Janice, who spotted a series of giant "bowl liners" made of man-
ganese that looked liked giant coffee cups without handles.
"Those could be planters," she said, at which point I had the
crane toss one into the back of my truck.

I dropped the "planter" in the parking lot, fetched two
more. I positioned the three planters in the parking lot and let
Jim know I was ready to go. He brought the dirt, and the plants,
and before things were even in flower I came into work one day
with a note slipped under the door, asking for a price.

I was immediately in the planter business, and Chessworks
has been shipping bowl liners ever since.

While the planter business has contributed nicely to the financial success of Chessworks, it was the plants that made the
statement. In later years I built a giant planter in front of the
shop. I fished the original bowls out and plunked a two thousand pound chess pawn in the middle, bearing a shiny stainless
steel flag that read "Art for Sale."

Jim has furnished that expanse of cracked asphalt with ba-
nana plants and giant thistles with bright blue blooms the size
of baseballs, and lantana, and whatever else has triggered his
imagination. I was so inspired by Jim's plantings that I started
my own honeysuckle collection. Jim dropped a wisteria into the
mix, with cautious instructions that it be pruned just so. His
garden contributions have transformed a non-descript building on the edge of a forgotten highway into a showpiece that
demands that drivers hit the brakes and investigate this fecund
roadside attraction.

In my latter years at Chessworks I routinely had visitors who stopped for seeds, or cuttings, and couldn't have cared less about the art.

Perhaps Jim is a customer. Or perhaps he is a partner. Over the years I have driven traffic to his farm. And over the years he has driven customers to me. When he added garden art to his annual sales event, I sold every piece I delivered, and he did not take the usual percentage cut.

I suppose that if someone were keeping a ledger of our transactions, I would be ahead. He has fed my boys popsicles, and he has donated plant material to the biodiesel co-op, and more importantly, he has inspired me to push on.

Once when I was shipping a giant chess set I had all of the pawns lined up such that they were peering over the edge of the truck. Jim popped in and suggested that they looked like "The Moncure Boy choir." I liked it. I made a piece called the Moncure Boy Choir, which consisted of twelve singing choirboys on a riser. It sold to a collector at a show in Maplewood, New Jersey. And it led to the fabrication of the Greensboro Boy Choir for a garden shop in downtown Greensboro. And it led to the production of the Sanford Boy Choir.

⬡⬡⬡

At the height of Chessworks, when I was shipping big chess boards throughout the region, and competing in sculpture competitions near and far, and staging openings with fair regularity, I brushed up against Don and Clyde.

Don was a lawyer turned artisan who ran a successful pottery with his partner Kenny. Clyde was a former district attorney turned real estate mogul who owned a big chunk of downtown Sanford. Together they were staging a pottery festival, which was an enormous undertaking.

They had television advertisements and potters from

throughout the region, and they had decided to do with pottery in Sanford what I had been attempting to do with metal sculpture in Moncure. We were a good fit. They had an eye on economic development.

And I had been at it for a while.

Clyde hired me to create some enormous sculptures for his buildings and install them downtown. My crew and I put the Sanford Boy Choir atop a three story building on Steele Street. And we made a series of giant toys that adorned the face of one of his buildings. One year those toys made the phone book jacket, as a defining Sanford landmark.

But Clyde's brilliance wasn't merely in commissioning substantial pieces of art. The deal he struck with me was that I would spend the money he paid in Sanford.

Which I was delighted to do. During those years, I took my crew to lunch in Sanford. My family rented videos in Sanford. I became a well-known customer at the scrap yard, and the local welding store.

I traded sculptures for large lunch tabs that could sustain a handful of us dining in style every day. When it was time for a fancy dinner on the town, I would book the window of the Italian place downtown and fill it with my family of six.

The deals Clyde and I struck made me a member of the local business community, involved me in the artistic revitalization effort, and caused me to re-circulate my money in the effort.

Mac and Jan opened an art gallery downtown and sold my work. We headed to Sanford for plays at the remarkable Temple Theatre, and we spent summer nights in front of the band shell kicking a soccer ball with the kids and listening to the local bands.

It was a wonderful and heady time. I was making a living as an artist, and playing the role in Sanford, and Sanford was thriving.

But the pottery festival never managed to surpass its big first year. Part of the problem was structural. Sanford built its convention center on the edge of town, rather than downtown where the revitalization was in full swing. Don and Clyde were successful at attracting thousands of out of town guests to Sanford, but they came to the edge of town, and left again, without spilling into the shops and restaurants and other venues.

Dollars collected at the festival itself left town the moment the potters closed their booths. And the event never went on to become the economic anchor that it was intended to be.

The five-star restaurant closed, and Mac and Jan folded up shop. A deathblow to the cause came when the city leaders closed Depot Park in the heart of things, for a two-year renovation.

Clyde sold some of his buildings, and the giant toys came down, and Sanford slipped back into Sanford as usual — which is an industrial town with an amazing scrap yard, and a vast amount of abandoned brick buildings.

The renaissance never really took, and Sanford — like Moncure — never really went on to become an artistic Mecca.

Nowadays I see Jim at the farmer's market. I recently started an evening primrose collection based on his offerings. I vanished into biodiesel, and he is still anchoring Haywood — just on the other side of Moncure. He has moved an old Post Office onto his lot and stocked it with an amazing collection of outsider art. His Haywood Museum of Art stuck — perhaps inspired in some way by my efforts to spawn an artistic recreation of the village.

It's hard to evaluate Chessworks as a project. From a financial prospective it was borderline. It did bring some artists to town. There was something to the SOHO effect, but it would be hard to describe Moncure as a vibrant community of artists — despite the signs the Department of Transportation

erected on three sides of the village, which read: Welcome to
Moncure, Community of Artists.

I spent about six years as a full time studio artist, and managed to build a sustenance for one person. Chessworks stood
for a decade, and remains a pleasant roadside attraction. Many
have fond memories of great parties and romances and pieces of
work gone by. And Moncure has become known for its artists.
But self-reliance is a long way off, and I am not sure where to
plug Moncure Chessworks into the framework of the possible.

I left Chessworks in the hands of Tuesday Fletcher, with
whom I have fabricated hundreds of sculptures. She is an accomplished welder, who stayed with me for the construction of
our biodiesel plant. She elected to close Chessworks in the fall
of 2007, bringing an end to a remarkable ten year run.

It could be that the soil in Moncure might have been too
thin for an artistic renaissance. And it could be the experience informed me. And caused me to head to the other end of
the road — to Pittsboro where there are more resources and
deeper cultural soils.

A Living for One

THERE ARE A FEW RHYTHMS to the Pittsboro-Moncure community, and those of us who have been around long enough plug into all of them.

One of the rhythms is set by BLAST, in which everything is electronic all the time. Another is set by a series of cell phone providers, the coverage of which tends to end on the Pittsboro-Moncure road. Whenever my signal is lost, I know I am getting close to home. The oldest rhythm is none of the above, and does not even include the telephone network.

Nobody telephones Wilbur the Woodman when they need firewood. The way we order a load from Wilbur is to visit him at one of his usual haunts. He might be selling pumpkins off the back of the truck at the dog wash on Hwy 87. Or he might see you at the Jordan Dam Mini-Mart and hand you more collards than your family could eat in several generations.

"Wilbur, I'm glad to see you."

"Good, good, how are you? Good, glad to hear it, good."

"We are cold Wilbur. We need a load of wood."

"I have some. I can get it to you. You know you are blessed to have a roof over your wood. Not everyone has that."

"Can I get two loads?"

After which you wait. He might come the next day. He might come the next week. There is no tracking number, no "Thank You For Ordering" auto-reply, and no invoice. You pay Wilbur when he comes, and if you arrive home at night and find two glorious loads of wood stacked in your shed, you pay him later, when you see him.

I probably should note that I am a big fan of wood as an energy source, and have visited the subject many times in Energy Blog:

Revisiting Wood

These days we are anticipating cold nights ahead, and among other things, our thoughts turn to heating the greenhouse.

Last year we tried to fire a waste oil burner on vegetable oil and biodiesel, but we never got it working properly and lost a greenhouse full of bedding plants. It was heartbreak, and a big setback for the farm.

This year we have decided to install a woodstove. Firewood is something we have in abundance, and there are a bunch of us around who have plenty of experience heating with wood.

The other day I found myself in conversation about North Carolina's electrical mix, and I mentioned the 4 megawatt wood fired generator over in Craven County. I always include them in my thinking because they are the state's largest renewable energy installation.

And I was cautioned not to think of wood as renewable.

Whoa. If wood is not renewable, we are in deeper trouble than I thought. I know it is fashionable to think of trees as "the lungs of the planet," but as someone who heats with wood, I prefer to think of them as batteries. They sequester the carbon, which I release with fire, to keep my family warm.

I spent one summer in the timber business. After Hurricane Fran decimated our place, I built a swimming hole with a couple of friends. My role was on the chainsaws. I would liberate twelve foot rounds, and skid them up into piles, which we would then ship to market.

I would fetch one price for a load of southern yellow pine which would go to the construction markets, and another price for a load of gum which would go off to pulp and paper. My highest dollar load was hickory, which went off to be made into pallets.

Most of America's hardwood goes into making pallets. We need pallets to ship "stuff" around on.

And as anyone who has ever run low on firewood knows, pallets make for great heating.

Call me old fashioned, but I'm going to leave wood on the renewable side of the energy ledger...

One of the people who operates on the same wavelength as Wilbur is Screech. He lives at the Bus Farm on the Lower Moncure Road, and the way to do business with Screech is when you bump into him.

Screech is an accomplished builder of greenhouses. He helped build the one down at the Land Lab at our local community college. And he has rescued more than his share of derelict greenhouses over time. He built our greenhouse at the biodiesel co-op, supervising some volunteer energy along the way. On the surface, with his grey beard, ponytail, and distinctive voice, he does not appear as an "expert." But he is. He's an experienced expert who is also a man of action. I have done a handful of transactions with Screech, and all of them have come to fruition.

One time I found myself at the Pittsboro Farmer's Market without enough money to pay for my large bag of wares. I sheepishly turned to Screech, who was selling lettuce off the back of his truck, and he agreed to pay for my market run. He took the top off his coffee can and fished out twenty bucks.

"Thanks, Screech — you know I'm good for it — at least this early in the month..."

The day Julie threw in the towel on her and Leon's hardware business, she called my cell phone. She was exiting the hardware business to open a florist shop a few blocks away, across from the County Jail.

"The fire sale is on, Lyle, you go down to the store and pick out what you want and come talk."

I took the call on Hank's Chapel Road, on a Sunday, while driving the Dodge pickup truck into town to do some work. I was glad to be in the truck, and glad for the diversion, so instead of swinging by Piedmont Biofuels Industrial, I headed for Julie's abandoned hardware store.

When I arrived I found Screech working in his greenhouse, which had long stood in Julie's side yard. I was delighted to bump into him since I needed a tractor moved. He has a big diesel pickup, and a big trailer, both of which exceed my trailer moving capacity, so I started the conversation by seeing if he could move a tractor for me.

He seemed demoralized. He was spraying bleach out of a spray bottle onto rough cut two by fours.

After we came to terms on the tractor move I said, "What are you doing anyway?"

At which point he launched into a long tale of woe. I knew he was an expert on greenhouses, and I knew he sold "rabbit food" at the farmer's market, but I did not know his story.

Screech is a heating and air conditioning man by day. He read a book once that said there was money to be made by growing hydroponic lettuce. He wondered about that. It caught his imagination so hard that he resurrected Julie's greenhouse and gave it a try.

The business went something like this: Check the plants in the morning on the way to work, check them again at night, and come in Saturday morning to move the plants around.

Screech played the game for awhile, started producing some beautiful lettuce, took out a stall at the Pittsboro Farmer's Market, and was off to the races. He developed some loyal customers, produced a miraculous product, and was well on his way to testing the book's assertions that a profit could be had through this activity.

It all looked like it was coming together, until the Town of Pittsboro passed by and sprayed herbicide in the ditch right next to his greenhouse. The intake fans on his greenhouse vacuumed up their poison and destroyed his crop. And his business.

When I bumped into him he was starting over. That meant replacing every poisoned pipe, and trough, and spraying things down with bleach. He was not in high spirits.

"Why don't you move in with us, down at the biodiesel plant," I said. "We have room for you, and we don't spray."

"I can't. Julie owns part of the greenhouse," he said, dejectedly.

At which point I drove down to the florist shop. Julie is a former model who used to appear in suntan oil ads. She is beautiful, and smart, and appears to have been in business all her life. When I showed up at her new florist shop I said, "I'll take the greenhouse."

She smiled, and indicated that she could not sell that because of Screech, who was a co-owner. I explained that I would buy her share, and jump in with Screech and all that was involved in that.

And I offered her a dollar.

"Lyle, you know I love you, but this isn't about love, this is about business. I have money in that greenhouse, and I need it back."

At which point I asked her how much she needed. To which she replied. To which I responded, to which she agreed.

I left her florist shop, ran down to the instant teller, came back with a stack of twenty dollar bills, and became the proud owner of Julie's share of Screech Owl Greenhouse.

Screech wasted no time. He tore down his existing greenhouse and moved it over piece by piece to our biodiesel plant. He erected it — with some help from volunteers along the way — and he was back in business again, almost overnight.

He put his coffee can in the corner, and showed us how to cut lettuce on the honor system. On some occasions, like big lunches in our shared kitchen, we would enter the greenhouse and nip a handful of giant lettuce heads.

Screech started selling to Chatham Marketplace. And to passersby who came to the plant for meetings, or tours, or for fuel. And we were all enamored with his greenhouse hobby.

One of my favorite things about his operation is that he pumps the CO_2 from his outdoor propane heater into the greenhouse, where it serves to enhance plant growth. He claims his heater is 99.97% efficient.

On two different occasions I have had engineers and agricultural experts visit and study the lettuce greenhouse in awe. They would mumble about ambient CO_2 levels, and mutter that this wasn't possible. On both occasions I was thankful that no one told Screech he couldn't grow hydroponic lettuce like that. If they had, perhaps he wouldn't have done it.

Other visitors claim to have seen similar systems in Holland, or in other far away places.

I find that is often the case with energy. In North Carolina we inhabit an energy backwater, where innovation is hard to find, and where our energy literacy is exceedingly low. In the renewable energy crowd, therefore, most of the talk about what can be done is based on things that are allegedly being done elsewhere.

"They are doing that in Germany," or "I've heard they're doing that in Brazil," are common catchphrases, which more times than not turn out to be largely exaggerated or false. Screech's greenhouse is surely referenced in thousands of conversations by now — after all we take dozens of visitors through it each week. But I am afraid that his innovative sequestration of CO_2 will morph into "...they're doing that in North Carolina." The fact that it is one remarkable HVAC man in one amazing greenhouse will tend to get left out of the stories.

That's merely an energetic sidebar to the tale of the greenhouse. Screech had some sales. He was up and running, and looking good, and putting out more lettuce than he could sell.

And then Sandi ran into trouble. She's the woman who runs ECO Organics, which is across the street — also inside the gates of our plant. She had run out of products to keep her customers happy in the dead of winter. She went over to Screech's greenhouse, lopped off a couple of heads of lettuce, and drove them over to her customers on the other side of the lake.

They approved. At which point she managed to buy every ounce of lettuce Screech could produce. He's recently doubled his greenhouse — in part because he likes selling lettuce off the back of his truck — and in part because Sandi has suggested she will buy all the mizuna he can produce — as long as he separates it by mature shoot and baby shoot.

Nowadays it is not unusual to see Screech trudging across the street with ten pounds of product piled high in wax boxes, to be dropped off on a refrigerated truck and sent to market. His is an amazing success story that serves as an inspiration to anyone who sees it — or better yet to anyone who bites into his wares.

⬡⬡⬡

Another remarkable tale of business success is that of Cathy Holt. Cathy was an accomplished metalsmith. She had a picturesque house over near the lake, surrounded by woods in all directions. It was hard to find, but that was the way she liked it, since her one room shop was packed with gold and silver and other valuable items.

That's not true, exactly. She kept most of her raw materials stashed in the broiler beneath her stove.

Cathy was renowned for her workmanship and designs. She made bodices out of precious metal that people wore as pendants and broaches. And she maintained a reputation that was slightly larger than our town. Her work was carried by high end galleries in far away places, and revered by local women. Those who longed for a Cathy Holt original had to get in line.

Decades of jewelry making took their toll on Cathy. Maybe it was the metal she ingested in her home studio, or perhaps the constant hours spent hunched over her worktable, or it could have been the repetitive motion of grinding out brooches, and earrings, and endless pieces. Whatever the cause, she found herself hurting, and was forced to abandon her profession.

What do you do to reinvent yourself, when you have been self employed all your life; you are approaching middle age, and can no longer ply your trade? If you are in a small southern town in the Bible belt, where people prefer sweet tea to alcohol, it is obvious that the first thing to do is become a yoga instructor.

Cathy was a successful artist, but I'm guessing she had lived a life of modest means. She does not come across as either poor, or rich, but comfortable in the middle. And when she rented a room at the Episcopal Church, to hang out her shingle for her first ever yoga classes, I worried about her.

My relationship to yoga had terminated in high school. In my teenage quest for self knowledge, I went deep into both yoga and transcendental meditation. My practice led to the cusp of receiving coffee enemas, at which point I started casting about for another religion.

When Cathy was embarking on her new career, I was interested in being a progressive employer, and I wanted to lavish my people with benefits.

We had a volleyball court, and lake views, and ping pong tables, and a corporate culture that included bicycles and fishing poles propped up against people's desks. I was on the edge of Research Triangle Park, and I was competing for talent with vastly larger companies, so I attempted to buttress my employment packages with massive flexibility and a compelling corporate culture.

Yoga was perfect.

I asked Cathy to offer classes inside our company. I pledged to deliver her minimum class size in order to make it worth her while, and in the early days, I took a spot from time to time to ensure the success of the project.

I hate yoga.

I was never so glad as the times there were more than enough employees, or others, to fill her early classes.

And fill her classes did. She filled up the church space, and she filled up our space, around the time that yoga came into its own. Cathy started her new venture before *Yoga Magazine* was on the rack at the supermarket checkout line. Her startup was before "hot yoga" or "power yoga" became so popular, which means she managed to catch the yoga wave at a very good time.

Tami immediately became a devotee. As did my brother Mark. Lots of people started signing up for Cathy Holt Yoga.

The good news was that I was off the hook. As classes filled up she no longer needed me to make it worth her time to drive across the lake. Lots of people started showing up for yoga.

A couple of years later, I needed to leave my beloved schoolhouse, with its empty gymnasium. It was time to move my business into Pittsboro, and we built a new building behind the Post Office. And when I was planning it, I asked Cathy if she needed some space. The building went up, and in the middle was a strange classroom sized space that had its own entrance, and its own bathroom, which was rented by Cathy to house her thriving enterprise.

That meant I got the children on yoga night. And my employees chastised me as a yoga drop out. So did my friends. A social class divide emerged in which there were those who did yoga with Cathy, and those who did not.

I did not. Which made me the subject of ridicule. I countered with the idea that "Yoga is what's wrong with this town," followed by a more defensive, "yoga wrecked my life."

The reality is that Cathy's ability to re-invent herself from metalsmith to yoga instructor is in part a measure of the health of our community. We had enough people willing to pay for something new that Cathy was able to make a go of it. It's as if our soil was deep enough for her business to take root.

⬡⬡⬡

By the time Tarus landed in Pittsboro he was already in the big leagues of the narrow and specialized field of network monitoring. He and his big brain had traveled throughout the network management community, and he had settled on the value of "open source" software.

One of the underpinnings of the Open Source movement is that the source code is available for free. Rather than buying a software package to complete your task, you simply fetch the open source equivalent you need for free.

Network monitoring is not free. It's ungodly expensive. Which means that when Tarus rented an office in Pittsboro to set up his "free" software enterprise, he was a bit of an anomaly. He is a six figure guy who would have been delighted to open his new business at his country estate, where he has "a bunch of expensive horse flesh in the front field," but he could not get the requisite bandwidth in his part of the Chatham County woods to do the job.

So he rented an office on Hillsboro St., Pittsboro's equivalent to Main, and went to work. Along the way he encountered BLAST. He noticed when he called BLAST he got a human on the phone. That was different.

Tarus probably has more experience with telecom than most people in Chatham County, and he became intrigued by the small town Internet provider.

Not only could he get a human on the phone, he could get the CEO to lunch at the General Store.

And so began my education in Open Source. Tarus brought his OpenNMS project into BLAST, and for awhile I was selling accounts for him. The only one I landed was the British Broadcasting Corporation, for which Tarus gave me a wonderful golf shirt with a logo embroidered on the sleeve.

He and his project passed through BLAST and he ended up renting space down the hall. From a cultural standpoint, he needed another six figure expert. And another. And another.

He filled his space with highly paid experts who travel the world offering consulting, delivering code revisions, and upgrades based on free source code.

Talk about Small is Possible. The mightiest corporations on earth turn to a five person software company in Pittsboro for their network monitoring using OpenNMS.

Open Source is funny. The bank president finds out that the ATM in Syracuse consistently leaves the network, and he is tired by the customer complaints. So he tells his information technology (IT) staff to get it monitored. The IT staff is watching its budget like a hawk, and had not included network monitoring in their plans. So some genius in the basement corner, goes out and fetches a copy of OpenNMS, figures it out, bolts it to the network, and viola, network monitoring is now in place.

The bank president is delighted, when he sees that all of his ATM machines can be automatically polled and monitored, and he says, "Fantastic — how did you do that?"

"I did it with Open Source software, sir. It's free."

At which point the bank president flips out because he cannot run his enterprise on free software. He needs support. He wants to be able to get an expert on the phone.

Which causes the IT genius to call Tarus to see if he can buy a service contract. Which Tarus happily sells him.

With a maintenance agreement in place, the bank now has confidence in its network monitoring, and rolls out OpenNMS to division after division.

Which simply feeds Tarus' business.

He can troubleshoot, he can answer questions, he can recompile code, and he can support the free software, for a price.

And he can add new features.

The giant network management company calls and says, "We have evaluated your software and found that it does eighty five percent of what we want. If it just did "this" we could roll it out across the enterprise."

At which point Tarus quotes them a price to add the functionality they need. They agree to buy it, Tarus does the work and ships it, and the new feature is added to the code. Which means the next user gets it for free. The first one pays for it. Everyone else gets it for free.

And the product gets stronger.

Another aspect of Open Source is that developers jump in when they find the work challenging. They like puzzles. Sometimes they are paid by giant corporations, and their contributions to improvement of the product is part of their job, sometimes they are moonlighting, working on source code for hire, and sometimes they are merely passionate.

What it means is that a small firm like OpenNMS can have way more developers working on their project than they could ever actually afford. IBM sells network monitoring software. So does HP. Firms like that require massive development staffs to keep shipping features to market fast enough.

Tarus espouses the philosophy of "release early, and release often," which means he also pushes new features to market. The difference is that his new features are either paid for by customers, or contributed from the community, so that he can stay in the game with the big dogs.

Eric Steven Raymond wrote a cornerstone book on this subject entitled *The Cathedral and the Bazaar*, from which Tarus routinely quotes. It is hard not to put it down without thinking that Open Source software makes all the sense in the world.

During my time with Tarus I joined him at the Triangle Linux User Group, and I met some of the players in the Open Source industry, and I learned a tremendous amount, but instead of staying in the software game, I moved on to biodiesel.

And when I did I infected our project with the idea of being "open source."

Something in the human animal wants to be proprietary and secretive. We have developed a culture that encourages patents as a road to wealth. And along the way we have forgotten that the more power we give away, the more powerful we become.

It's all back to John's therapy shack on the edge of his pond in Silk Hope. When the start point is that you get everything you want or something better, there is no need to keep secrets.

In our journey through biodiesel, Rachel, Leif, and I have had myriad opportunities to pocket valuable knowledge with the idea that we might somehow parlay that into huge financial gain. And instead we have pushed our knowledge out to the world. We've done it in blog entries and through public presentations, and through our extensive website. We've made our information free, and as the result, we are perpetually hired as consultants in the biodiesel field.

One day David and I were hired to consult on a farm-scale biodiesel plant. I met with the Fire Marshal and worked on permitting issues. David worked his usual design-build magic. As we were driving home in late afternoon, I reflected on our insanely high daily consulting rate, and it occurred to me that Tarus would be proud.

As a Wikipedia contributor, I jumped in on the entry about Tarus and added the idea that his thinking on open source had a powerful influence over the entire grassroots biodiesel movement — but as is often the case with Wikipedia — those contributors who are more interested in network monitoring overruled my contributions.

But it is true that Tarus provided me with an education in open source, and that our project found itself committed to open source from the get-go, and that it wasn't long before others in grassroots biodiesel were sharing the open source philosophy.

As is frequently the case, as soon as the thinking moves into the incomprehensibly large, whether it is proprietary or open source, the picture becomes muddled and bewildering.

The fact is that Tarus can compete with IBM and HP on network monitoring. OpenNMS can employ a handful of experts, and manage a community of developers, from Pittsboro, and in doing so can provide above-average wages and standards of living along the way.

We find the same principles at play at Piedmont Biofuels, where we are continually paid for our work in education.

It works something like this: Matt Rudolf gets hired to do a presentation on biodiesel side streams in West Virginia. He delivers the work, gets paid, and gives them the presentation to publish online, re-use, whatever. Next month Matt Steiman hires us to drive to Pennsylvania to do a talk on side streams for the home brewer. I take the West Virginia presentation, add everything I know about the subject, and deliver it in Pennsylvania. I get paid, and publish my talk in Energy Blog so that the whole world can avail themselves for free. Rachel then comes along with an order from the National Center for Appropriate Technology (NCAT) for a curriculum. She realizes she will need a segment on biodiesel side streams, so she grabs the work from Energy Blog, adds her touch, and sells it to NCAT.

NCAT says it is the best piece of work they have ever seen and wants to publish it in companion publications and push it out for free to anyone in the world who might need to do a presentation on biodiesel side streams. Rachel says, "Fine, all we ask for is attribution," and the content enters the world again.

At which point my phone rings to see if I would be interested in doing a paid presentation on biodiesel side streams based on the material the caller saw from NCAT. The cycle continues, the work gets stronger, and that which is "free" gets paid for over and over again.

Whether it's the studio artist, the lettuce grower, the wood man, the yoga instructor, or the network monitoring guru, at the heart of a vibrant economy is a meaningful living for one.

Economic
Re-Development

W HEN EMJ NEEDED to leave Triangle School, I went shopping for real estate. I drove around Pittsboro, looking at buildings and lots to try to figure out where to move my enterprise. It was an intense amount of pressure. The phones need to stop ringing at one location, and start ringing at another — right on time. And employees tend to locate themselves around work — so every move threatens dislocation, and every dislocation can lead to the loss of people.

In my twenty-five years in business, my people have always been my most important asset. I've never held a patent, or invented a widget, or had a business that could stand on its own with simple "labor." All of my businesses have been dependent on bright people with good ideas and the ability to work hard. Which means that every time I lost one, my business was set back.

I hate moving businesses.

But my landlord doubled my rent, and I figured I could build a building for less money. When I told him that, I think he thought I was bluffing. I never learned how to bluff, so I was on the road with my company again.

During my search I came across a strange little property on the edge of town. It was locked up tight, surrounded by barbed wire fencing, with a guardhouse that had a turnstile that would let people out, but not in. The "No Trespassing" sign was from Inco Alloys.

Honeysuckle was taking its toll on the fence, but through the weeds I could see a number of strange looking buildings. I wanted to explore.

So I headed to the office of our Economic Development Corporation, which is a nonprofit agency run by Chatham County Government. At the time it was run by Tony, who was a silver haired fox of a man who lived in Southern Pines, drove a large car, and regularly staged golf tournaments for the captains of industry around town.

With my payroll numbers, Tony frequently interacted with me, and often invited me to his country club functions. We both knew that we were approaching the world from different vantage points, but our relationship was cordial — and he was always very helpful.

I would write Internet posts and articles bashing our county's economic development strategy, accusing them of chasing smokestacks and being completely wrong-headed in their approach, yet whenever I needed help from our Economic Development office, they offered it up freely.

On this occasion I wanted a key. Tony had a key. He handed it to me, along with an aerial shot of the property. "It's not for sale," he said.

I ran back and opened the gate, which slid on giant rollers, via gravity, as if the place had been waiting for me.

And I wandered around. There were four steel and concrete buildings with hinged metal roofs that would lift up in the event of an explosion, and fall back down into place again.

There were giant hydraulic presses, and a mezzanine, a small office and a warehouse.

The place was creepy. And magical. It was at the end of a gravel road, surrounded by woods, completely fenced, and the buildings were unlike anything I had ever seen.

Try as I might, I could not visualize how to move my technology company there. I needed office space, and this place had cavernous hallways with giant metal blast doors.

At my schoolhouse, I had grown accustomed to daylight, and a lake view, and I could not conceive of how to wedge my company into these four bizarre buildings.

The loss of employees would have been too great.

But I did hunt down Inco Alloys in West Virginia, and I did learn they were interested in selling the property. They had around a hundred acres, and wanted a mere million dollars. That was outside of my snack bracket, so I passed on the project.

Instead, I bought a ten-acre lot behind the post office with two beautiful ponds. I found a design build firm in Sanford and laid out a remarkable north-facing building with geothermal heating and cooling, an expansive front porch, a day lit warehouse, and a bunch of other energy conservation features which made it unique.

But as the design work was coming to an end, I left the family business. After fifteen years in a computer industry rowboat with my brothers, I decided to set my oar down and climb ashore. My departure sparked anger, and emotional discharge, and relief. And when it was over, I found myself free to pursue other interests. I believe the normal lie they run in the papers is that someone is "leaving to spend more time with his family."

I left to open an art studio.

One of the photographs I pinned on my bulletin board in my new studio was the aerial shot of the strange little alloy plant on the edge of town. It had lodged in my imagination, but there was nothing I could do with it.

The experience did color my thinking, however. It made me think our Economic Development Corporation was flaccid. Had they been hustling, they would have known the building and land could be purchased. In fact, they would have had it listed by a local realtor.

Along the way I learned that the property *was* highly valued by our tax office. So highly valued, in fact, that it was more important than my payrolls. Large capital investments are better for the tax base than jobs. We value capital more highly than people. I was employing engineers, and professionals, who thought nothing of paying a premium for a high-quality sandwich at Mimi's General Store, and I thought *that* was the straw that stirred the drink of the local economy. I was stunned to learn that it was less important than 100 acres of abandoned real estate that was endowed with expensive motor controllers and presses and concrete walls. It was an early indication to me that we had something horribly wrong in our economic value system.

Years later, I returned to the beautiful EMJ building behind the post office, and found myself watching the kingfishers and herons hunt the ponds. As I worked I watched snakes get plucked from the grass by hungry raptors, and I enjoyed watching the turtles bask on fallen logs.

The building was fantastic; my return to it was painful. I had left my sculpture business and re-entered the world of the Internet. I was back into corporate life, as the new CEO of what became BLAST Internet Services Inc. I was bored out of my head, and making some biodiesel on the side, and as I failed to upright the failing Internet business, biodiesel grew from a hobby to a co-op, and from a co-op to a commercial concern.

Years had passed, and I went back to the alloys plant. Tony still had the key. The property hadn't budged. The land had passed to a new local owner, who was busy building an industrial park in Siler City.

I walked around again — this time with an eye to a chemical plant. I no longer needed beautiful views for knowledge workers. This time I needed space for tanks, and a mezzanine, and I needed the big water, and big sewer, and big electricity that came with the place.

I was so jazzed by my second visit that I immediately grabbed Leif and Rachel, my partners in biodiesel, and brought them out for a walk around. Before walking the abandoned campus, we had no intention of opening a commercial biodiesel facility. But it was hard to walk through so much abandoned infrastructure without imagining a million gallon per year operation. The place made us feel like it was completely possible.

Leif and Rachel fell in love with the spot instantly, and my marching orders were to raise the money so that we could break ground.

For that I went to my brother Mark. And others. And in no time we had cobbled together enough money to buy the land and what we thought would be enough money to get a commercial biodiesel plant built.

I left my Internet CEO position, and took a seat in the abandoned control room of an abandoned alloys plant in January of 2005. I found a metal frame with peeling lead paint, tossed a board over it, and with the help of BLAST, figured out how to get a telephone working over the Internet.

We had about twenty thousand square feet of strange space. I selected the original control room because I thought it would be out of the way of construction. It had no daylight, and no fresh air. It was not insulated, which made it both hot and cold, and nasty.

Leif pulled in with a used table he fished out of another building, and took a seat beside me. Evan arrived on project. We found him a desk somewhere. And the three of us were wedged into a horrible space where the air seldom moved. When Rachel left her job at the Community College, to throw her hat in with us, we had no room for her. Matt and I came in one weekend. I fired up my oxygen and acetylene torch and cut a hole in the control room wall that expanded it to a utility room beyond.

Rachel's space was just large enough for a desk and a bookshelf, and we referred to it as the Hobbit Hollow based on the curvature I had cut in the door.

We lived in that space for about a year. The Control Room housed three telephones, four cell phones, and a fax machine, and it was so cramped we had to go outside to change our minds. It was misery.

But our presence in that space began the re-development of that space, and we have managed to transform it from a strange White Elephant on the edge of town into a fecund and magical space. We now have seven different businesses inside the fence, from our commercial biodiesel plant to a charitable foundation to a hydroponics greenhouse. The place has gone from dormant to bustling.

And I still chastise our local government officials on their economic development strategies. I published an article in the Chatham County Line in February of 2007, which went something like this. It got me into trouble with the new local political machine:

Forget the Elephants

Chatham County's economic development has been characterized by chasing smokestacks around. And it's a shame that we don't tend to catch that many.

When I try to remember the big industrial catches over the past fifteen years, I find most of them got away. There was the steel recycling plant that was designed to munch up cars in Moncure. Didn't happen. There was the landfill — largest on the Eastern Seaboard — also for Moncure — but folks didn't want that one. There was the mental hospital for Siler City. That went to Butner. Drat.

We did manage to land 3M. It is the last plant 3M will operate in America, and it came here. Whew. I am fortunate enough to live across the road from the 3M lands, and am pleased to report that all it cost us was our night sky and our silence. Now when we weed our gardens we do so against a constant background rumble. The sales of white noise machines must have plummeted at the Jordan Dam Mini Mart after 3M came to town.

It's too bad we haven't been able to land more factories. We've staged plenty of golf tournaments, and lunches at all-you-can-eat buffets, but instead of landing industries, we tend to get housing developments instead.

Funny how that works. When you are a bedroom community you tend to attract a lot of bedrooms. Since people spend their money where they work, those who merely sleep in Chatham spend their money somewhere else. When they spend their money someplace else, our community is depleted. Which means our past economic development approach has been entirely wrong-headed.

Instead of putting our money on ideas, and small business (where most new jobs are created), we have been out hunting for elephants.

Instead of investing in water and sewer and vacant lots in hopes of catching some "industry," we should invest in bandwidth so the affluent folks who pass through town when it is dark on their way to work, could stay home and telecommute. That way they might head to lunch in town, or figure out that we have a local hardware store where you can get actual answers from an actual human being.

Instead of throwing a golf tournament for the captains of industry, we should be backing Chatham Arts or the Studio Tour. Economic development should encourage the creative folks who pass by on their way to and from work to spend some money in our midst.

Or better yet, we should invest in incubators and shared office space so that these people can actually work in Chatham.

My wife Tami was inspired by such a vision. She's been wholly engaged in small business in Chatham for the past decade or so, and when she saw there was an opening for an Economic Development Officer, she floated her resume. She doesn't golf. She's obsessed with local economy. And anyone who has ever worked with her will confess that she could sell gravel to the 3M gravel pit.

Fortunately for me, our new political machine passed her by. It seems that the good folks at the Chatham Coalition and our fresh new board of commissioners prefer out-of-town talent.

Instead of re-inventing our economic development strategy, they have elected to hire UNC to consult with us on these important matters. Please. Hiring UNC, that bastion of status quo thinking up the hill, to help us with our economic development is like hiring a consultant to read our watch to tell us what time it is.

It's time to change our thinking. It's time to shuck business-as-usual and do something different. The smart money is on sustainable agriculture. And clean energy companies. And co-ops. We should be insisting on zero-emission homes. The smart money is on ecotourism — and tourism in general.

I wonder what the economic development incentive package was like for Shakori Hills. Whenever they throw their festival of music and dance, our county is packed with visitors. People spend their money where they visit.

If we want Chatham to be a vibrant and prosperous place to live, let's not discharge our sewage into the Haw River — people come from all over to shoot Gabriel's Bend in their kayaks and canoes. Let's start valuing our night sky, and our clean air, and our quietude. Today these assets are less important to our tax base than a bunch of abandoned buildings — most of which have been left behind by an industrial era that moved away a long time ago.

Let's accept that our economic development strategy to date has been a failure, and that any new approach should transform our community from a place to lay our heads to a destination for work, entertainment, the arts, and small business. Forget catching an elephant.

The elephants moved to Indonesia a long time ago.

I have since found myself at odds with our economic development folks over and over again. I suspect my problem lies in the fact that I don't know anything about "economic development." Because "economic development" is different from doing business.

In business you form useful relationships that can assist you to grow. You provide value propositions for customers and vendors, and work tends to be performed in the name of mutual benefit.

"Economic development," on the other hand, appears to be government's way of appearing to be in the business game. It involves the publishing of reports, and the facilitation of conversations, and the need for more study. From what I can see, our government continues to put out ideas long after business has figured it out.

I once attended a presentation by our Economic Development Corporation that indicated that if we wanted to, we could form "clusters." These would be groups of businesses that would trade with one another based on feedstock requirements. The co-products of one would be the feedstock of another, etc.

Really? I wonder if that is why the feed mills located close to the chicken factory. I wonder if that is why the processing plant located close to the growers of chickens.

Businesses do not locate in an area because of a paper issued by the good folks in "economic development." Businesses locate to their best advantage.

Good "economic development" is little more than an effective Rolodex. If the local economic development officer knows everyone, and knows where business resources are located, they could be of assistance to the business that needs such information.

"Business" needs a forklift to arrive tomorrow morning. Or an architectural drawing to get stamped to pass an inspection.

"Business" needs a trucking company to broker a load. Or a
builder who is competent. If government could provide this information, there would be a value to the business community,
but unfortunately most Economic Development Officers don't
even reside in the community which they serve, which leaves
their rolodexes without any pertinent life.

Which leaves them largely useless.

Occasionally "economic development" means the successful relocation of some giant firm. This is often associated with
incentive packages that generally represent a simple transfer
of wealth from the taxpayers into corporate pockets. Michael
Shuman has written eloquently about the incentives game in
his book *Going Local: Creating Self Reliant Communities in a
Global Age.*

My take on the subject is probably best limited to the idea
that government should not have a toe in "economic development" in the first place. They should take the money they waste
with their studies and presentations and salaries and invest it in
infrastructure — like daycare centers, or bandwidth, or things
that would attract business people in the first place.

Main Street

DOWNTOWN PITTSBORO remains a sleepy place, which is mostly closed on Sundays. Liquor by the drink is not allowed by law, which means those establishments that sell alcohol have to sell food. Occasionally the downtown merchants will band together to stage a fish fry or show a movie on the wall of Antonella's hair salon — and there are occasions when the downtown pumps with life — but in general it's a quiet affair.

One of the merchant couples on Main Street is Jacques and Wendy. They run an import/export art and antique business called French Connections, a fascinating art and antique shop with an eclectic variety of imported goods. Large wooden hippopotamuses stand amidst hand-woven baskets, next to a mantle full of model automobiles made from Fanta cans in the developing world. Jacques and Wendy wholesale fabrics and wares, and are the composite merchants. On first pass, people would think that Pittsboro could not support a shop like theirs, but after many years in the community, the fifteen Eiffel tower models in the yard of their shop have come to define our town.

Jacques is a man of the world, who hails from the north of France, ran a textile business in Senegal, and settled in Pittsboro to raise his family. One night he shared his vision of downtown Pittsboro with me, and his insights formed the basis of my theory on "business succession." Just as the softwoods grow fast and die young, to be succeeded by the slower growing hardwoods in the forest, the downtown business landscape evolves.

Today the main street of Pittsboro is largely populated by real estate brokers and insurance agents, which have little to offer after hours. They will give way to art galleries, and antique shops, and specialty businesses as the value of real estate increases downtown. The low-margin service businesses will make way for the high-margin retail businesses as the town's population increases, and can support more interesting shops.

Which is not to say we lack interesting shops. Across from the courthouse, looking out on the traffic circle is a hand wrought John Amero railing leading up a few steps to the front door of Beggars and Choosers.

This "vintage clothing" store is the brainchild of Pam Smith, who has been buying low and selling high at the same location for decades. If one were to perform a Wikipedia search on "colorful character," I'm confident Pam's picture would emerge.

She's a colorfully dressed southern woman with a thick accent and a twinkle in her eye. The first time I encountered Pam was at a Robin and Linda Williams concert at St. Bart's Episcopal Church on Salisbury St. They would play a song, and she would holler and hoot at the top of her lungs. It wasn't halleluiah, exactly, but it sure felt like it. It was enough to make the polite Canadian in me recoil in embarrassment. She was soaking up the songs, and shouting out her enthusiasm.

I have no doubt the story of Pam and Snuffy Smith would make for a delightful book in its own right, but for now they are simply players in the local economy. Beggars and Choosers is renowned. It draws customers from far and wide; some come for silly costumes, some come for furniture settees.

I once flirted with a large advertising agency in Chapel Hill. They talked of acquiring my little Internet company. I was stunned to learn that their founder — an erudite and fashionable man — bought his furniture exclusively from Beggars and Choosers.

Before there was such a thing as "ecommerce," I tried to sell Pam a website for her shop. When we were talking about it, I heard she acquired a collection of heirloom jewelry and clothing, pushed it out onto the fledging world wide web, and flipped the entire thing to the Smithsonian.

Pam and Snuffy throw house parties that are legendary, during which police involvement tends to be limited to directing traffic. And at the same time, whenever Beggars and Choosers holds a "re-opening" event, all of downtown comes alive. It might be a player piano in front of the shop, or a manikin likeness of Marilyn Monroe, but whatever the stunt it draws a crowd.

Her shop is a local institution that has helped put Pittsboro on the map. Tami and I are not consumers of vintage clothing, or art deco saltshakers, but we tend to invest heavily in Halloween — the costume time of year. Before Chatham Marketplace existed in physical space, we held a "masquerade" at our house that drove heavy traffic to Pam's store. And each year Piedmont Biofuels celebrates Halloween heartily.

I joke with Pam that we keep her in business. She's good-natured enough to play along, but she doesn't really need us. She has built a property that has endured. And anchored our town.

Across the street from Beggars and Choosers is the locally owned Capital Bank. They used to be the Sweet 16 sandwich shop, which served a credible milkshake, but a night deposit box has replaced the cutting boards, and the milkshake maker gave way to a safe. Presumably they were knocked out by the growth of the General Store Café across the street. Capital would be just another boring bank, if they did not bake cookies onsite and offer them to their customers. And if it wasn't owned by area businesspeople.

At the end of the block is S+T's Soda Shoppe, run by our former travel agent, Vicky and her husband, Eugene. These two ran off to Hillsborough and bought an historic pharmacy, which they moved, piece by piece, into a building in Pittsboro.

From the perspective of atmosphere it is nothing short of amazing. The ornate wooden pharmacy shelves, and the booths with embedded mirrors are remarkable. When you pull into a booth and look around, you can almost see the early twentieth century pharmacist offering up a prescription with a soda.

Apart from a typical "heart stopping" North Carolina menu, which is backstopped by food off a truck, the Soda Shoppe has worked on how to be "customer facing" in its approach. I used to eat there, before switching to my hundred-mile diet, and they were kind enough to put out white vinegar in glass flasks to accompany their French fries. That was a nice touch. One any Canadian can respect.

For the longest time, the building next to the Soda Shoppe was Edward's Antiques. Tommy Edwards is a local singer/songwriter and an anchor player in The Bluegrass Experience. Cindy is the merchant in the family. She's a historian and pottery collector. The two ran a successful antique business for many years. Cindy now runs the Arts Incubator in Siler City and remains a pillar in the local business community.

The many antique stores of Pittsboro come and go. They are at once treasure troves for seasoned collectors, and pawn shops at the same time. When times are tight, you can load up Uncle Charlie's manual Underwood, take it door to door around Pittsboro, and come home with some walking around money. When times are good, there is a chance it will still be sitting in the window, and you can buy it back for more than you paid for it.

When your back goes out and you need a cane, the many antique shops offer a remarkable selection.

Across the street is Pittsboro Appliance, which flies the black POW/MIA flag. Archie served in Vietnam, and has been peddling appliances from his corner shop for as long as most can remember. His service is second to none. If you pop in to buy a microwave oven for the lab (to keep the interns from warming up biodiesel samples in Tami's custom kitchen), Archie is likely to engage in a conversation about your last washing machine.

"I would have liked to have set that back foot just right, but the floor on your porch is so weak, I just couldn't get it set right."

Anyone who wonders how it is Archie's business is still thriving, even after the big name appliance vendors came to town, needs to merely stop by each establishment. One is a franchise in a strip mall, with a powerful brand and an overworked manager who is operating by the book. The other is Archie, who is one part salesman, and four parts customer service. Those who predicted that Archie's business would end when the big box retailers came to town have not bought enough appliances from Archie.

Next to Archie's is Van Finch's survey office. Surveyors and lawyers populate our Main Street, since we are the county seat and they must interface with the records office. Realtors, lawyers, surveyors, and their clients comprise the lion's share of our pedestrian traffic on most days.

Across the street is Elizabeth's Pizza. It's a local chain, run by Hispanics. I believe it was founded in Elizabeth City and has been working its way westward. Their pizza is far superior to the over-formulated, petroleum based pizza offered by our local pizza chain stores.

In this snapshot of our Main Street merchants, I have omitted some by accident, and others by intention.

Pittsboro, like many small southern towns, has a convergence of cultures that is reflected in our mix of local businesses. We have the old guard. If you are interested in racist jokes, you can head to the barbershop, where aging white men miss the days of old.

Or you can head to the Scoreboard for Shag dancing lessons and a goodly helping of secondhand smoke. Many of our businesses are split along tobacco lines. Those that allow smoking post warning signs that smoking is allowed.

We have plenty of right-winged, non-environmental, get your hands off my business, homophobic, preserve-the-status-quo small-business types — in fact they dominate our local Chamber of Commerce. And we have plenty of merchants like Catherine at New Horizons, who sells funky footwear, garments, and gifts to the "nutty crunchy" crowd.

Economics is tied to point of view. I have a couple of little boys, and I don't cut hair. For awhile I was in the market for what I will call the "little boy haircut." This is before they took up skateboarding, and before they understood the Mohawk hairstyle, and back when a simple haircut was a fatherly decision that was merely implemented by whichever vendor could deliver the service.

Off to the barber shop we go, and the next thing I know I am having to field questions about the meaning of the "n" word.

Got it. We needed a new purveyor of the "little boy haircut."

Which we found. Our choice of haircutters was driven by convenience, and price, and values; but when the fast cheap haircut downtown came loaded with "values" from yesteryear, we moved to less convenient, more expensive options.

Perhaps racism is like the fast growing pines, and homophobia is like the fast growing gums, and both will make way for more tolerant oaks, and hickory trees. I'm hoping Jacques' vision of business succession is right. Today our Main Street is partway there.

PART II

Homegrown

Homegrown is all right with me
Homegrown is the way it should be
Homegrown is a good thing
Plant that ell and let it ring

NEIL YOUNG
AMERICAN STARS'N'BARS
1977

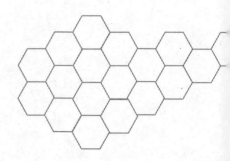

Connecting Ourselves

Local Internet

I WASN'T THE ONLY ONE who almost missed the Internet. The big telephone companies did too. Dialup access should have rightfully been the domain of the giants, like AT+T or Sprint. Because they were asleep at the switch, new giants, like AOL, emerged. And perhaps more importantly, tiny little Internet Service Providers (ISP) sprung up everywhere.

One of them emerged inside my corner of the family business.

Scott had worked with me at EMJ for many years. He was a brilliant technician and a gifted programmer. I had encouraged him to moonlight, I had landed him some "outside work" that was not on my company's dime, and I had escorted him into the computer industry. In turn he escorted me into the Internet.

When Scott came to me to explain the future, I yawned. We would sit around after hours with core employees and argue about the coming of the net.

One night, our sales manager, Skip, said, "Travel. Let's take travel. How do you buy your travel right now?"

I thought of Lisa, the preacher's wife turned travel agent, who matched up the itineraries of Tami and Lyle like a marriage counselor scheduling appointments, and I answered Skip's question honestly:

"The other night I came out of my bathroom, and found my travel agent at the kitchen table cutting up a lime on the cutting board. She had let herself in, and had brought over a box of Corona beer.

"I sat down, grabbed a beer, and she told me that tonight we were going to get clear on whether or not Tami and I were going to Belize or Jordan. Tami came home late from work, grabbed a beer and settled into the conversation.

"Are you telling me that one day I will replace that with a computer screen?"

I humored Scott and company, and bought them some bandwidth, and lent them equipment, and encouraged them to throw themselves into the new venture. They charged off into the world to start a new Internet business, stubbed their toes, and came back looking for work, with a thick business plan they had written.

It looked like fun to me, so I bought their company, tucked it into EMJ, and in no time I found myself in the rapidly growing Internet space. In the beginning I traded websites for office furniture, and for roasted peanuts, and in no time we were kicking out gigantic websites for corporate America.

When it was apparent that we needed to move the business, I made it clear we would be moving closer to my residence in Chatham County. It was my third move for the business, each one chopping time off my commute.

Steve McConnell was an employee who had become a friend. He was an avid bicycle enthusiast, and used to ride for hours on the back roads to and from work.

"If you are looking for a place to move," he said, "There's an old schoolhouse on the edge of the lake which would be nice."

Triangle School was an interesting project. When Chatham County Schools was forced to integrate the races, the schoolhouse became a casualty. It had new life for a moment when it became a parochial school for the Seventh Day Adventists, but fell back to abandonment. As it sat empty, the Army Corps of Engineers came along and built Jordan Lake. There are no buildings on Jordan Lake. Except this one, which could not be occupied because the lot could not support a septic system.

I went out to look at it immediately. Possums and poison ivy, graffiti and the remnants of homelessness greeted us. Vandals expressed their dissatisfaction with the educational experiences they had there in a variety of interesting ways. Anyone planning to come back to this world in his or her next lifetime should note that an abandoned schoolhouse is a rotten choice.

I immediately fell in love with the place, and when confronted with the septic issue, I went down to NC State University in search of a solution. There I found Dr. Hal House, who devised an indoor-outdoor constructed wetland that could be built in the courtyard such that the building could process its own waste.

With a septic solution in hand I bought the building. But when my board of directors in Canada found out they were afraid I had violated some Security and Exchange Commission rule about purchasing real estate without public notice — and I was forced to sell the building immediately.

I sold it to Nate Schaffer, who had a booming neon sign business located in a reconstituted hatchery in Pittsboro. Nate was a builder. And a blower of glass. He went to one trade show one time, to display his handiwork, and he came home with a decade's worth of work. In the beginning his business did custom neon signs for bowling alleys and bars, but as he expanded into the schoolhouse, he ratcheted up his output and started blowing Miller Lite signs for the German market.

He renovated the building, and built the constructed wetland, and I lived there with my company as a tenant. From my perspective I had a five-year lease that would auto-renew every five years into perpetuity. It turned out to be an incredible space that I loved. We could see the lake from our conference room; we built a volleyball court out back. We ran a pair of ping-pong tables in the warehouse where you could always get a competitive game.

As an experienced beer drinker, I wondered about Miller Lite signs for Germany. I spent a couple of weeks in Germany each year, and I could not imagine why anyone in Germany would ever order a Miller Lite, or why any bar in Germany would want a Miller Lite sign for its window. But Neon Impressions was just another little company like mine, plugged into the global economy like me, so I shrugged off the questions which occasionally crossed my mind.

At Triangle School I had twenty-five people employed on Internet, and another twenty-five employed on computer distribution. When combined with the nineteen people of BLAST, I ended up on the upper echelon of a Chatham County Economic Development Corporation list of local employers. I had become a big fish in the little pond of our local economy.

With my reduced drive time, and my ability to lunch locally, and especially with my mini bully pulpit as Mr. Technology Employer, I started noticing local issues.

One of them was Chatham County Schools. North Carolina ranks poorly in national ratings of public school systems, and Chatham County ranked poorly in North Carolina. My travels through the Internet landscape made me an evangelical believer in point casting. Rather than broadcasting content to people, I saw a world in which each person acted as a point and fetched their own content at their leisure.

And I wondered if the concept might help in our schools. Down at Chatham County Schools I met Dr. Larry Mabe. He was an intriguing fellow. He was well-educated, and loved to shed his southern accent to speak French. And he was well-paid — perhaps the highest paid county official at the time. As such he was a target for criticism and had many detractors.

I found him intriguing. And more importantly, I found him to be a man of his word. He made decisions quickly, and stood behind them. When I suggested that we pull an Internet connection into every classroom in the county, he agreed.

We started with Moncure School. I mobilized employees with expertise. He brought in other businesses. The brick factory sent a team over to the school, and we fished wires through attics together. Other companies donated money to the effort to pay for spools of wire. Blast took charge of Horton Elementary, and knocked it out. My firm wired Northwood High School. Parents showed up to help. And when we were finished, there was a working Internet connection in every room.

Our work together drew headlines and awards and for a brief moment we shifted the perception of Chatham County Schools. We operated well together. I provided some contract expertise, Dr. Mabe became a customer, and together we put Chatham County Schools on the technology map.

On one occasion I suggested that the school system could become its own Internet service provider, and that he could offer access as a perk to his many employees. There was an ISP in Raleigh that had folded, and I acquired its gear for pennies on the dollar. Dr. Mabe liked the idea, said he would buy it all, and I drove across the lake to get it. On my way home the cell phone was ringing from other ISPs who had got wind of the purchase and were making me offers at a higher price, but I had a handshake agreement with Dr. Mabe, and delivered the gear to Chatham County Schools.

At the time Chatham County was a long distance call to anywhere. By opening a local point of presence, our Internet business was able to provide a subscription service without long distance fees, and as a business model, it thrived. We were providing access, and web hosting, and assembled an amazing staff of artists and designers that produced remarkable work.

I sold the company to the employees, just as the Internet "bubble" was starting to expand and they rode a remarkable wave for several years. Like many other Internet firms, they came back to earth hard.

After ten years of struggle they never managed to retain enough earnings or retire enough debt to stand on their own and prosper. They did build a remarkable wireless network which still sends bandwith through the woods. Scott cobbled together an amazing collection of gear, and communication paradigms which are still alive today. At one point he transmitted his signal off the water tower in Pittsboro, caught it at a house on the hill in Moncure, sent it back to a jerry rigged tower at the biodeisel co-op, and re-distributed the signal from there. At one point the plan was for me to catch the signal at my house, send it across the creek to Bret's place, where Bret would pass it along to Jan, etc. Today many of us still rely on Scott's network for email, web access, and voice services, although his company is much smaller than it was in its heyday.

He remains the technical genius that he has always been, although now he tends to conduct his business from his back porch — or from the solar powered shed he and Rachel built in their back yard. From there he can put his feet up and watch the packets fly by on the network he created.

Feeding Ourselves

Chatham Marketplace

MELISSA FREY is a fierce warrior in her own right. I'm not sure how she came by her power, but when you are in her presence, it is inescapable. She is a widow, with two kids, living in Bynum, which is a little abandoned mill town on the Haw River just north of Pittsboro.

She volunteered at Weaver St. Market in Carrboro — which is a legendary co-op grocery store — and she dedicated herself to the task of opening the same in Pittsboro.

It turns out she topped Weaver St.

Weaver St. is an established food co-op, which has been highly successful at building not only its brand, and balance sheet, but also the community in which it resides. It has spawned cooperative housing projects, and a community radio station, and it has become a remarkable anchor for the Town of Carrboro.

To their credit, the folks at Weaver St. wrapped their arms around Melissa as Chatham Marketplace took shape. Somewhere in the Co-op creed is the idea that startups should get an assist from the established, and Weaver St. Market did just that. Instead of worrying about competition, or about whether or not they would lose valuable organic food eaters if a new grocery store were formed, Weaver St. Market lent a hand to Chatham Marketplace.

Their founders offered free advice, and they had a feasibility study on a Pittsboro location sitting on the shelf collecting dust, which they passed along.

Weaver St. freely gave power away to Melissa, and as a result they became more powerful. Now Chatham Marketplace exists in the world, and for that Weaver St. Market deserves a large slice of credit.

Melissa is another story. She is disciplined, and severe, and organized, and remarkable. When she started the idea of an organic grocery co-op in Pittsboro, she called a meeting in Bynum, which confused everyone from the get go.

Tami jumped in. She is the opposite of Melissa. She is agile, and lax — messy and adorable. When she latched on to the idea of a co-op grocery store in Pittsboro, everyone chocked it up to a dreamy pie-in-the-sky.

But the two did not let go. Opening the store was like shooting white water rapids, with a pair of guides who possessed largely flat-water experience. They hired a consultant, and they put out a table at a thousand events. Chatham Marketplace was at the Pittsboro Street Fair, and the Shakori Grassroots Festival of Music and Dance, and at the Chatham Arts Council events, and on and on. They sold memberships in a dream, and people bought them.

In order to open they needed not only memberships, but also low-interest — or no-interest — loans, and for those they beat down the doors of the community. They formed a board of directors — John, Laura, Corrine, Kathleen and Tes — which they deputized to twist arms and make calls and pump up the dream.

Kathleen was an expert marketer who was entering motherhood. John worked for Celebrity Dairy, and was an energy expert. Laura came from the sustainable farm community. Corrine was a local accountant. And Tes was finishing her doctorate.

Combined they may not be accurately called a "rag tag" bunch, but I think it is fair to say they represented a checkerboard of past lives.

Some were drawn to the project by a hunger for organics, some by sustainability, and all were driven by a desire for local selection. After all, for those in Chatham County who care about organic food, Weaver St. Market is a long drive.

Together they worked booths, and spoke to community groups, and posted to message boards, and made phone calls through the dinner hour. Together they raised a big chunk of money through memberships — people who had essentially pledged to eat their food — and another big chunk of money through loans from individuals — people who were less interested in seeing a return on their investment than they were on seeing a cooperative grocery store come to town.

When they had sold 500 memberships, and raised 350,000 in community loans, they had enough collateral to borrow a half million dollars from the national co-op bank in Washington, DC. With a million dollars in hand, they set out to create their store.

Securing a location was another story. That was not a small feat in Pittsboro in 2004. The Chevrolet place was available. It had a terrific parking lot, and a location everyone would see, but it was essentially an abandoned singlewide that was paneled with the tar of many years of tobacco smoke.

There was the old post office on Salisbury St. It was off the beaten path, but was about the right size. Its owner was complex, and was more interested in selling the building for a vast sum than leasing it to a fledgling market concept.

There was Emergency Apparatus, which was behind the General Store. It was a dream location in many ways. Chatham Marketplace could move in behind Vance, and let him front-end the lunch crowd. That way the new grocery store could compliment his efforts instead of compete with him. There were visions of a bakery, and nighttime shopping, and harmony all around.

An added plus would be the removal of Emergency Apparatus. That was a company that hopped up fire engines and other emergency vehicles. Their main claim to fame, apart from the George Bush stickers on their vehicles, was that they had successfully leased the parking lot behind the Blair Hotel. Once they had their lease on the asphalt, they strung chains about the place, and rented spaces to business owners in the cramped downtown. They hung signs on each space, indicating who was allowed to park there, and suggesting that others would be towed.

When no one saw it happening, the lot reverted to its public status — only with chains and signs strung about.

Emergency Apparatus is the dream small town business. Almost all of its customers come from out of town, and leave their money in our midst. As a specialty shop, it evolved into a niche that allows it to survive and prosper. The only problem is that its success was most commonly denoted by big trucks blocking traffic, or the privatization of a previously public lot, or with occupying all of the great space behind the General Store.

The perfect place for Chatham Marketplace, behind the General Store Café, was filled with fire trucks in various states of repair.

In the background of the quest for space was Chatham Mills. In its day it was a great producer of woven labels. Mill-workers in that building sewed the labels that went inside the sweaters and pants which North Carolina shipped to the world. The mill's silver water tower is what greets people entering our town from the north, and it could surely serve as a trophy model for something out of a Garrison Keillor talent competition.

The mill is enormous. Great wooden beams span dramatic spaces, and little square single paned windows surround the place. Tom, who keeps his office in a little white house on the property, which is surely a vestige of the mill town gone by, is the owner of the place.

Restoring abandoned mills is a North Carolina real estate tradition. We were once dominant in textiles with an industry powered by rivers for cheap electricity, and uneducated workers for cheap labor. Textiles moved to the developing world a long time ago, leaving us with hundreds of abandoned mills — almost one in every town.

Nowadays mills become condominiums with river views, or shopping centers full of retail activities. And restoring an old mill is a terrific way to go bankrupt. One of our closest models, the Carr Mill in Carrboro, which is home to Weaver St. Market, has bankrupted two previous owners prior to arriving at the vibrant condition it finds itself in today.

To Tom's credit, Chatham Mills has not taken him under. Yet to a disgruntled community, which perpetually envies the empty space, the mill has not been brought back to life fast enough. For over a decade it has sat on the edge of town, mostly empty. And like any empty building, it depletes the energy of passersby.

Every now and then a tenant will emerge. UNC Health Care. Or a dialysis clinic. While the public wants the place to bustle with brewpubs and theatres and art galleries, a biotech firm will move in, and no one will have any idea what it is they do.

As the result it is a complex property. Tom is cautious. Careful. And he is slowly renovating additional footage as he goes.

His dialog with Chatham Marketplace has followed a similar pattern. While it was clear from the outset that Tom's mill was the place for the new grocery store, his approach to managing the property was ill suited to the fast paced, dreamy concept of a cooperative grocery store.

Which means the quest for space went from the mill to the old post office to the mill to the Chevrolet place, and back to the mill, and so on. Often the process was fraught with strong personalities, solemn oaths never to deal with one another again, and promises that were impossible to keep.

Melissa stepped aside to let Tami take over the real estate part. Sledd Thomas stepped in, too. Tami had the experience with landlords, and real estate deals, and is known for her ability to not only negotiate, but also to sell. Andrea jumped in. She took a job working for Tom with the express purpose of getting a grocery store opened in the old mill. And eventually a deal was struck, and a lease was signed.

Before the space had been finalized, the Board of Directors recruited Mary to manage the impending store. She moved to town with a yappy dog named Brutus, and an abiding passion for co-op grocery stores. Mary grew up in the countryside of New York State, in a large family. She remembers burning an incandescent light bulb all night long to help keep her room warm.

For a time she was operating the marketplace out of her rented house. Wine merchants would come to town and she would invite the board, and others over to sample their wares. She was setting up vendor relationships, and recruiting staff, and planning the store from her kitchen table. And she worked with Tom on getting open.

By the time our fire marshal passed Chatham Marketplace for its final inspection, most of the sparks and fireworks had already passed. The screaming had come to an end, the tears had dried, and at long last we had a new grocery store in our midst.

When its double electric doors opened on the edge of the mill, it was clean, and bright, and it smelled good.

Talent flocked to the store from far and wide. Tim put his broadcasting career on hold to become a cheese monger, and set about educating our community on various cheeses — including instructing producers on packaging and selling their products. Jeff the Chef emerged from the woods and assembled an inspired delicatessen and hot bar. He launched a blog in which he proffered recipes, philosophy, and coverage of marketplace life.

While getting open was a monumental task, staying open kept the challenge alive. In order to hit their projected numbers, they needed more eaters. Or they needed their core eaters to buy more products.

And so the board, and staff, set about the long journey of twenty thousand "tweaks." Dave came in and kicked the sandwiches up a notch. They got rid of the slow moving items, and replaced them with the things people want. They collected suggestions, and went to work.

An early survival strategy was "events," and the thinking was they would pack the place for special occasions. But each event needed to be approved by Tom, and Tom was not inclined to authorize events carte blanche. A cumbersome approval process, which was built into the lease, left the event strategy hamstrung.

One event that took root was the poetry slam. Local poet Geoffrey Neal took charge and made it shine. Tami went out and bought a public address system. And the place filled up with poets, poet wannabes, and lovers of verse. Kids piled in on the front end of each event, and whenever a poetry slam was held, the day's receipts climbed closer to the break-even point.

A catering business was launched. With a full kitchen and deli, supplying food to the hot bar, a logical follow on was to figure out how to project their services to remote locations. Like the grand opening of Piedmont Biofuels. Or to Anne's sixtieth birthday. In the dramatic struggle for each day's number, occasionally a catering gig would make the difference between profit and loss.

In-store marketing took precedence, with samples of products and vendors setting up to sell their wares. And an education campaign was launched. Kathleen held a seminar on how to buy from the bulk section. An all-out push was made to knock people out of their patterns, to try buying new things.

Melissa was dislocated from volunteer "founder" to a paid marketing position, and in that capacity she launched a remarkable newsletter, in which disparate voices wrote about their involvement and perspective on Chatham Marketplace.

Shortly after the opening the word spread through the community that the prices were high. I had been asked to write an article for the *Chatham County Line*, a small newspaper that invites authors to tackle a specific theme each month. They were soliciting articles for their "Local Business" issue just as the "high prices" rumor mill was gaining speed. I published this article:

The Free Hand of the Marketplace

After years of persistent energy, Chatham Marketplace is at long last opened for business in Chatham Mill several blocks north of the Chatham County courthouse on 15-501.

This community now has a locally owned and operated place to buy groceries, which has at its heart, the idea of making local produce and wares available to its customers.

That may sound simple enough, but providing a local marketplace in a global economy is an exceedingly difficult thing to do.

At the heart of our market thinking is the idea that consumers will always act in their economic self-interest, and will always procure goods from the lowest cost producer. In our current world, that can leave our local economy in shambles.

Since North Carolinians can no longer compete in textiles, we watch as our textile industry moves to far away places that can deliver cheaper wares. First textiles, then furniture, and on and on such that our country's manufacturing days are rapidly fading into a carbon coated sunset.

Although we can put up protectionist trade barriers, and cry foul over working conditions and lax environmental regulations in our competitor's lands, the reality is that this is how we like it. The free hand of the market is working great. It is in our best interest to get cheaper goods, and voila, we are awash with cheap stuff.

Enter Chatham Marketplace. With its thirty new jobs, and it's roughly four thousand square feet of renovated retail space, it's now jumped into our local economy and is ready for trade.

Like all the other consumers in the free market, my self-interest comes first.

I like the fact that their milk from Maple View Farms is cheaper than the milk at Food Lion.

What I will pay for a product is one consideration, and I have others that influence my purchasing decisions. A central factor for me is time. If I can get the product I want quicker, my self-interest is better served. Since my travels mostly include Pittsboro, I find Chatham Marketplace to be a tremendous time saver. In the free market that we cherish, time is money, which makes time almost as important to me as the price of the product.

Another critical consideration for me is fuel. Since I drive around exclusively on B100 biodiesel, which is more expensive than petroleum, I tend to watch my fuel consumption like a hawk. Included in everybody's price for groceries is the cost of fuel.

Since I am in business in Chatham County, a strong local economy is good for me, which is why I try to purchase my goods and services locally. Dollars spent in an economy tend to circulate around and around before leaving town. The other day I went into Blue Sky Equestrian, which has recently opened downtown. A sticker on the door referred to this circulation saying, "Buy Local. Spend it Here, Keep it Here."

Monetary circulation is commonly measured with a "multiplier." The multiplier is a number that counts how many times a dollar travels through our local economy before heading for some place else. Chatham County's multiplier has been steadily dropping during my brief sixteen years here. When we once boasted multipliers of 7, and 5, we are now seeing multipliers of 2 and 1.9.

That means that when I used to go to the local hardware store, where I would spend a dollar, that same dollar would travel from local vendor to local vendor seven times before ending up in the cash box of someone far away. Today, if I spend money at J. Henry, or

Carolina Hardware, the chances of my dollar being spent again in town is pretty high.

If I head out to Lowe's on the bypass, however, chances are good my dollar will leave town immediately, where it will circulate in someone else's economy.

This concept is at the heart of NC Plenty, a local currency that circulates out of Carrboro and includes Pittsboro in its limited geographical area. It makes sense that Chatham Marketplace accepts the Plenty at face value.

Local businesses, like Chatham Marketplace, offer a chance to trap dollars in our local economy, and by re-circulating them to local growers and merchants, there is an opportunity to enrich us all. The other day I joined Mary (Chatham Marketplace's manager) on a trip to Lindley Mill near Eli Whitney. They mill complete lines of organic flours, and spelts, and sell them for less money than Wal-Mart.

Other consumers will have other considerations that influence their grocery buying habits, and those people will also find Chatham Marketplace serves their best interest. Some may be interested in food that is organic, or natural. Others may be consumers of supplements.

Selection will also drive buying decisions. One night when dining on the porch of Chatham Marketplace, I heard a patron quip, "It's the best sushi between here and Jordan Lake."

The other day, when a friend of mine was loading up on Celebrity Dairy goat cheese for an impending road trip, I bumped into Farmer Doug, who had recently dropped off a load of cucumbers. His cucumbers are grown in Moncure, which is about ten miles away.

He picks them, and delivers them to Chatham Marketplace. When I buy them there, take them home and serve them, I can still taste the day's sun.

No need to shrink wrap. Or to store them on refrigerated trucks. Not a lot of imported petroleum went into their production or delivery to market. Doug's cucumbers are merely a delightful stop-gap before our own cucumbers fill the back garden.

Last night as I was leaving Chatham Marketplace with some beer that was brewed in Asheville and some meat that was raised in Silk Hope, I bumped into Eric Henry from T. S. Designs. He's an apparel merchant from Burlington. Eric is making a stand in the textile trade by selling organic cotton products that are made in America. Rather than close his factory, he has retooled his business to address the "sustainability niche." He was unloading boxes and boxes of product which have been successfully selling at Chatham Marketplace.

As I headed for home I could not help but reflect on how "it's working." Years of planning, and raising money, and meeting, have paid off. Consumers who value products from our local economy, from early cucumbers to t-shirts, are now able to get them conveniently in Pittsboro.

Which is exactly the way a market is supposed to work.

That article helped change the message, and objections to higher prices died back. Almost a year later, Lauren filled a typical shopping cart full of random products at Food Lion, and the equivalent basket full at Chatham Marketplace, and found the market commanded a thirty seven cent premium.

Mary took the occasion to send a brilliant email to the membership:

Dear Fellow Chatham Marketplace Owners,

What is 37 cents worth to you? Keep reading and see what it means to your store...

First, "Thank You" to the almost 500 of you who filled out our recent survey. We received a great wealth of information about what we are doing right and about areas that are ready for improvement. We've already begun working on your feedback...keep your eye out for positive changes!

One of the most surprising responses we received is that 85% of you do 50% or less of your weekly grocery shopping at your Co-op! One of the main reasons expressed for not doing more shopping here is that Chatham Marketplace is seen as too expensive (here comes the 37 cents). I encourage each of you to reevaluate this perception.

Yesterday, Lauren did a shopping cart comparison with a Pittsboro conventional grocery store. She chose 35 items, from milk and eggs to cat food to toothpaste to bacon, and found that the TOTAL difference for this shopping trip was only 37 cents. Wow! (Send me an email if you want the comparison!)

That is 37 cents which stay primarily in Chatham County. That is 37 cents which supports and encourages LOCAL milk, eggs, flour, produce, meat, soap, coffee, beer, ice cream, bread and more! That is 37 cents which provides 30 people jobs, which they are proud of and enjoy.

That is 37 cents which keeps YOUR store OPEN.

Chatham Marketplace needs you. We are here for you and because of you and we need to be your main grocery store.

This is your Co-op, let's make it a success.

Please don't hesitate to contact me for any reason!

Cooperatively,
Mary

In many ways the story of Chatham Marketplace is a story of messaging. Melissa said she was going to do this, and Tami believed her. Others bought into the vision, and as long as the message has been, "This property will get open," or "Our prices are not higher," the project has progressed nicely.

On one occasion the board of directors freaked out about the financial situation. Monthly losses were piling up, and the message from the primary fund raisers switched to: "We can't raise money in good faith for a project that could close tomorrow."

That message reverberated through Mary and into the staff and out to the suppliers, and in no time everyone expected failure. I heard about the impending failure from a truck driver who was dropping his load at ECO Organics.

Just as despair was settling over the project, the Abundance Foundation stepped in. They are a local non-profit that is focused on local food and renewable energy. They bought a slicer for bread, and another one for meat. Mary needed them to increase efficiency and to expand the range of products the deli crew could offer. At the time the store was losing tons of money. The board had lost sight of the vision. There was no money for new slicers.

Tami went to work on getting control of the message, changing it first to "Fantastic, only 100,000 dollars more to lose," and then to "Closing is not an option." She followed up with the delivery of two new slicers, and morale began to swing. At the time, Tami was nearing the end of her term as Board

President, and had taken a job as the Executive Director of the Abundance Foundation.

Perhaps a successful grocery store, with expanded product offerings, could prosper. The soil of the community was healthy enough to provide strength to a seedling store. The slicers came as an amendment — a symbolic donation that showed a fledgling foundation was in the Marketplace's corner.

The new message was not about failing. It was about getting everything that was needed — or something better.

Mary introduced a discount day, which was named "Ten on the Tenth," in which everything in the store was ten percent off list price on the tenth of each month. Price conscious shoppers emerged from the woods, and receipts on that day began to steadily climb. Past the daily break-even total. Past the two-day mark. Onto sales that could cover a week's worth of revenue.

Tweaks continued. Everybody pulled. Customers forgave bugs in the system. Some investors forgave their interest payments. Suppliers modified their systems to accommodate the needs of the Marketplace. Donors bought picnic tables, and Tami lined the porch with exquisite scrap metal art tables by Janice Rieves. Real estate developers bought large blocks of memberships, and started giving them out as closing gifts.

And with each passing week the numbers got stronger and stronger. Still laden with debt, and by no means out of the woods, the story of Chatham Marketplace is a remarkable tale of one woman's vision, which became a group endeavor, which is an ongoing community work-in-progress.

It surely takes more than a marketplace for a community to feed itself. It takes growers, and vendors, and producers of all sorts. But along the way Chatham Marketplace adopted policies and tenets that have underpinned its way of doing business.

And buying local is at the heart of the project. With a newly added local meat section, and a hot bar that is largely prepared from local farms, and with locally produced buying preferences exercised throughout the store, it currently boasts a thirty percent local content number.

That compares to Whole Foods, which is roughly six percent local. Which compares to Food Lion, which is closer to three percent. North Carolina is a vast producer of food, after all. On the global commodity markets we trade punches with Iowa for first place in terms of poultry and pork production. We are growers of soy, and makers of pickles, and while we bemoan the loss of tobacco, agriculture is the largest industry in our state.

Which means it would be hard to open a grocery store in North Carolina and not find some locally produced products on the shelf. Three percent is an ambient rate. Like background radiation, it will be there.

But to rise above that takes work. In a food system that has become industrialized, it is hard break the mold. Even Weaver St. Market, which is beyond reproach on so many levels, falls victim to "the California Price," which pits local broccoli producers against a global economy.

And that tendency can also be seen at Chatham Marketplace. In a property that will not fail, buying from local producers can be a challenge. Small producers can be quirky. Quality can be erratic. Food handling and storage systems can be substandard. And in an economy where it is cheap and easy to get fine looking food — even fine looking organic food off a truck that has traveled thousands of miles, there is a tendency to follow the path of least resistance. The overwhelming need to move perishable product quickly and easily can drive a store's decisions.

With a foundation rooted in local economy, Chatham Marketplace has largely managed to check that desire, and stay wedded to its tenets. Its local selection has actually shown signs of increasing over time. Fancy beers with corks from Belgium have started being displaced by local microbrews. Cheeses from Holland have declined, and cheeses from local herds have increased. Locally made hot sauces are replacing those from Louisiana.

Chatham Marketplace is working.

Growing our Own

When you walk through the red clay of North Carolina, it's permanent. It will color your boots, and your doormat, and your floor and your rug. And in Pittsboro, sustainable agriculture acts in the same way. If you walk around town long enough, you are going to brush up against it, and when you do, it will stick with you.

It might be a conversation with a red-clay booted stranger in the General Store, or it might be when you hold the back door of Chatham Marketplace open for some farmer who is pushing an overloaded hand truck of produce. It could be a charity dinner, in which you are seated next to one of the many staffers of the local sustainable farming organizations. This town is full of growers, policy makers, researchers and eaters that are directly linked to our small-farm economy.

Many years ago Harvey Harman emerged from Bear Creek to teach what he had learned from operating Sustenance Farm. He started a sustainable agriculture program at the local campus of Central Carolina Community College.

He started with soils, and moved on to cover crops to protect the soil, and pushed deep into the field of permaculture. Tony and Robin joined him, and a "Land Lab," went up on campus. Farmer Doug stepped in and introduced us to "Community Supported Agriculture (CSA)," in which people were invited to buy a "share" at the beginning of the season, and show up each week to cart away a huge box of whatever he had to harvest.

I have been dancing with the "food miles" question for years. My journey toward the 100 Mile Diet started a long time ago, when I started wrestling with the issue. Often when I am wrestling with ideas, I push them out to Energy Blog:

1300 Miles Away

This morning around 5:00 A.M. I crossed my fingers and started the Jetta in the dark.

I needed to deliver the kids to their respective air terminals and I had three vehicles on B100. No problem. Lucky.

We have just come off a week of feasting and playing and doing the usual Thanksgiving thing. Jess flew in from St. Louis. Dan and Kaitlin came from Des Moines. It was our usual expansion, bringing out leaves for tables and bedding for idle beds, wedging our family into this little farmhouse.

Amidst the ice-skating, and Risk playing, and between pinochle games, the discussion of local food began to loom large. They say the average American meal comes from 1300 miles away, and we chewed on that concept all week.

As always, the start point is math, and my fear thereof. Do you calculate the food by weight? Dan has no fear of math; in fact he is good at it. And he was all about figuring out the weights and percentages of each ingredient of the meal.

There was some objection to this methodology, however. Take stuffing. Jess and I got into a dispute about stuffing. She and Dan made one out of bread mix that came from Columbus, Ohio, with some spicy sausage that came from Tennessee. I argued that the sausage from Ray's General Merchandise in Moncure was superior, and made a special trip with Dan to prove the point. While there we picked up beer that came from Pennsylvania, and ice that came from Raleigh.

The problem with using weight as a determinant was illuminated by the sausage. Both were "spicy." Presumably if you left out the spice (a tiny percentage of the weight) you change the stuffing entirely — so much in fact that you might not bother with the dish in the first place.

This point was well illustrated by the inclusion of basil, oregano, rosemary and chives from the back garden. They made a nice contribution to the dish, but added little in terms of weight.

Chatham County has seen a bumper crop of pecans this year. We have been gathering pounds of them from a number of local yards and they have become a temporary staple. At the same time, Tami and I went to Siler City one day to procure ten pounds of chestnuts from a fellow I met on the Farm and Industry Tour. Roasted chestnuts were a hit right out of the pan, and completely vanished in the various stuffings.

Maple syrup posed another challenge. I did some maple-glazed carrots with pecans. I bought the maple syrup at a roadside farm in Ontario and carried it home after a trip to Canada. We have enough Canadian traffic passing through the farm that we never want for maple syrup. And while it is clearly not local, how do you score the miles for food that you carry with you?

Onions and carrots came from California — although we did have three locally grown carrots in the bottom of our CSA share.

Our weekly box of food is more than we generally can eat. While Doug's carrots are spectacular — too good in fact to glaze (we ate them straight or dipped in homemade humus), they were not plentiful enough to serve 15.

Our CSA did provide abundant sweet potatoes, greens, peppers and lettuce however, and at ten miles away it is hard to get more local than that.

As the local food discussion raged, Dan and I found ourselves digging through the trash to find container labels with addresses on them. Some were impossible to tell. White potatoes were branded by a distributor in Raleigh, but I suspect they come from much further away.

I dug some horseradish from the garden and made some cranberry relish with some spent sour cream and abandoned ranch dressing I found in the fridge. It was sort of a Mama Stamberg rip-off, based on ingredients I could find. Cranberries came from Wisconsin.

George stayed up one night and did a Turduckin — a boned chicken stuffed in a duck stuffed in a turkey and roasted together. When carved it delivers three colors and flavors in a single "slice." He got the birds whole at Cliff's in Carrboro — not sure where Cliff gets them from.

Flour for the biscuits came from Minneapolis, yeast and shortening from Ohio, salt marked from a distributor in Salisbury, with organic milk and butter from Boulder Colorado. By the time we throw in a bottle of wine from France, and olive oil from Italy, (which is about 5000 miles from here), I'm guessing that our meal is looking pretty average — at least from a distance stand point.

I need a way to score this meal. If I list the eighteen local ingredients as: sausage, ice, basil, oregano, chives, rosemary, pecans, chestnuts, carrots, humus, sweet potatoes, greens, lettuce, peppers, horseradish, turkey, duck, and chicken. And if I list the sixteen non-local ingredients as: sausage, beer, maple syrup, carrots, onions, white potatoes, cranberries, bread mix, flour, yeast, shortening, salt, milk, butter, wine and olive oil, it appears to be a pretty even split. Yet where we could lop miles off for next time leaps off the screen.

By now the children have changed planes and are re-entering their far away lives. It's a cold wet day that has progressed from simply depressing to positively dreary. I hang up some jackets in the front hall and notice that we are back to having enough coat hooks for everyone. I pull the leaf out of the kitchen table and wish every-one was still here for just one more game together.

Today our Sustainable Agriculture program is the only one of its kind at the Community College level on the Eastern Sea-board, which means it attracts students from far and wide.

They come to learn, and many end up staying on the land, breaking ground on small farms of their own. Chatham County is one of the few counties on the eastern seaboard that is seeing an increase in "on-farm" population.

But we need to be careful here. This is one of those sta-tistics that get bandied about that do not tell the whole truth of our situation. It is true that more farms are going in. The number of farm serial numbers issued by the USDA can easily demonstrate that.

But our farmland is vanishing. Our arable land is rapidly becoming golf courses and subdivisions filled with McMan-sions. Yet while the number of acres under cultivation is falling, the number of farms is growing.

People have figured out how to make a living growing ten acres of Belgian endive using techniques they have learned at the Sustainable Agriculture program down at the college.

Today our farms boast an astonishing array of small scale strategies that have proven to be highly effective — from slid-ing greenhouses for season extension, to hydroponics, to high houses to indoor fish farming.

Small growers who are shipping truckloads of mushrooms, tilapia, exotic produce, hormone-free meats, and fresh cut flowers dot our landscape. We have a vibrant sustainable food-shed.

In the midst of our growers are several formidable organizations that have sustainable agriculture at the heart of their missions. Pittsboro is home to the Rural Advancement Foundation International (RAFI), which is a highly regarded voice in agricultural issues, from feedstocks for biodiesel production to justice for farm workers. Their expansive headquarters is one of the first Energy Star-rated buildings in the state, and is a model of daylighting designed by famed local architect Alicia Ravetto.

While RAFI's headquarters are enviable, they are a couple of stone throws away from the offices of the Carolina Farm Stewardship Association (CFSA). It is wedged into the top floor of the dingy Blair Hotel, and boasts over a thousand members in the Carolinas. They have a gritty feel, holding conferences and acting as a clearinghouse for the many growers who seek their counsel. Anyone interested in grassroots advocacy efforts will find themselves impressed by CFSA.

Another important organizational presence in our midst is our Agricultural Extension Office, which is operated by NC State University. Although much of NC State is easily characterized by "big is always better" thinking — happy to improve the efficiency of a factory farm, or launch a monoculture of a new hybrid seed — they do have their toe in sustainable agriculture. They operate the Center for Environmental Farm Systems (CEFS) that is a sprawling operation in Goldsboro, and they employ Debbie, who is our local Sustainable Agricultural Extension Agent.

She is a tireless champion of workshops, and websites, and seminars on everything from bio diversity to fending off honeybee mites. Here is one of Debbie's typical emails:

Brace yourselves everyone...

The workshop season is in full swing — we just finished up an 8 week beekeeping school, plus two farmer conferences on heirloom tomato grafting and no-till vegetable production. Now my attention turns to three grant-funded projects including a biodiversity project promoting pollinator habitat on farms and developments (more on that later) and a farmer-to-farmer mentoring project. I'm now busy planning for upcoming workshops, trying to find time to work on the website, answer calls and emails, do farm visits...

On the street level of the Blair Hotel is the Rare Breeds Conservancy, where everyone from production farmers to hobbyists can get connected to animal bloodlines. The idea that underpins their mission is that vast monocultures of a single breed might be convenient, but it's foolish. Genetic diversity in our herds and flocks is a critical safeguard against disaster.

The presence of these three organizations alone means it is entirely possible to get an education on agriculture merely by stopping at the General Store for lunch. Whether it's an education on GMOs, or problems in the food distribution chain, or the economics of farming, sustainable agriculture is constantly present in Pittsboro.

At the heart of the sustainable farming message is the simple mantra of "soil, water, market," to which, in Chatham County we simply bolt on the addendum, "deer fence," and we are ready to farm.

That is, when we know what we are doing. Our red clay is rich in minerals but needs significant amendment in order to produce bountiful yields. North Carolina's Department of Agriculture (NCDA) provides free soil testing to anyone who sends in a scoopful of dirt. Their analysis is a start point for providing life to the soil.

Chatham is home to a pair of giant compost making facilities, which gobble up cardboard, and pallets, and sawdust and food waste from far and wide. As dirt makers these facilities combine trap-grease, wastewater, forest residues, and animal wastes in closely guarded recipes to kick out mountains of compost and topsoil.

Those in sustainable agriculture tend to turn up their noses at the commercially made compost, and make their own. At Piedmont Biofarm, Farmer Doug minds his piles closely, keeping them covered and with an internal temperature of 130 degrees. He turns them three times a week using "intern power." This management has two effects on the product: First, it could be certified organic. It's not, but it could be. And second, a hot pile kills seeds rather than providing them with an ideal place to germinate.

The compost I run in the garden off the back porch typically sprouts with tomato and melon seedlings, which means my product is merely a good way to move weeds around.

I once had the supreme pleasure of watching Doug and Dean discuss dirt over the hood of my tractor. I covered the conversation in Energy Blog, in an entry called "Dirt Snobs," in which I said, "Dean makes millions of dollars worth of compost each year. He runs a facility in Goldston that kicks out soil amendments for the entire region. He is one of the largest food waste processors in the United States. And he has been watching our progress over the years."

I went on to write, "No one makes better dirt than Doug. No one sells more dirt than Dean. Watching the two of them talk over a tractor was remarkable."

At the heart of their conversation were the whole egg shells that are evident in one of Dean's dirt blends. Doug's argument was that samples of Dean's dirt were found to be too high in calcium by the NCDA testing lab. Dean countered that egg shells offer a "slow release" of calcium as they dissolve into the soil and that NCDA does not take that into account in their lab sampling.

Dirt snobs like to be able to control the content of their piles. Cotton seeds, for instance, which occasionally arrive at the commercial composters in vast quantities, are often laced with the myriad chemicals required to produce cotton.

And there appears to be no limit to the distance dirt snobs will go when maintaining the purity of their soils. If I use a glossy magazine to ignite the kindling in my woodstove, are the wood-stove ashes suitable for my compost? Some would say not.

Wood ash is one of the amendments we crave. For the past couple of years, Doug has been seeking wood ash to turn into the fields of his sustainable farm. One year he blamed the size of his garlic crop on the inadequate supply of wood ash. Not being a dirt snob myself, I would have merely ordered a tandem load of high potassium dirt from Dean, so that the garlic bulbs could mature to the proper size.

Making soil is at the heart of sustainable agriculture, and for some it is at the heart of healing the planet itself. When Rachel decided to devote herself to changing the world, she figured the start point was to make dirt, which led her through the sustainable agriculture program at our local community college, and onto a farm of her own.

Our agricultural landscape holds traditional farms as well. Drivers through Chatham will pass cow-calf operations, and encounter chicken farms with vast chicken houses and tens of thousands of birds. Which means we have an adequate supply of chicken manure.

In his book, *The Long Emergency*, James Kunstler questions whether or not we still possess the vernacular knowledge to survive in a post cheap petroleum world. Since agriculture is one of the prime recipients of subsidized petroleum products — not just cheap fuel to operate tractors and equipment, but also supplemental nitrogen, herbicides, insecticides, and fertilizers of all descriptions — it is a sector of our economy that may very well not survive a transition out of the current mass-carbon consumption era.

But in the case of sustainable agriculture, Chatham County not only possesses the vernacular knowledge, it perpetuates it — drawing students from far and wide. I do occasionally wonder about "intern power." It strikes me that sustainable agriculture as it is currently practiced is excruciatingly labor intensive, and that "interns" who are on the sustainable farm circuit to learn the trade often provide labor.

I've heard Screech argue that the big sustainable farms are under-mechanized and use poorly paid interns to make up for the work that should rightfully be performed by capital-intensive machines. Screech is an accomplished grower, and greenhouse operator himself. He's in the hydroponics business — which is extremely energy intensive. But he does manage his operation without help, and he has been on the sustainable agriculture scene long enough that his opinions warrant attention.

I'm not sure which is correct. I see farm interns enjoying a high quality of life despite their low standard of living, and as an eater I enjoy the fruits of their labors. I also find they add a vital dimension to our community.

Water is becoming increasingly hard to come by in these parts. Many of the models scientists use to predict climate change has the southeast of the United States showing up as a loser on the global warming front. We have experienced drought for four out of the past five years, and all the forecasts indicate that we need to learn to live with less water.

I once went up to the University of North Carolina to see Hunter Lovins speak. She waltzed onto stage, just off the plane from Afghanistan, and started her PowerPoint presentation. At one moment in the middle of the talk she interrupted herself, looked squarely at the audience and said, "I understand you folks are experiencing a drought again this year." Then she shrugged, and said, "Get used to it," and went on with her presentation.

For me it was a horrifying moment. Drought causes severe background stress on our family. Because our well has been known to sputter dry, we need to be exceedingly careful about watering decisions, and normally at the peak of the dry season we find ourselves deciding between life and death. I will offer a bucket of waste water to Ruby's gardenia. But the camellia is going to have to make it on its own.

At the beginning of the gardening season we are dedicated waterers, and our plants flourish. Pleasant cool nights in the garden call for more plant material, propagation of favorites from last year, and an uncovering of perennials that we had long forgotten about. And our season follows a predictable pattern.

The cool nights of spring give way to sweltering summer, when the garden fills up with ticks and poisonous snakes, and we lose our enthusiasm for the whole affair. Water shortages merely exacerbate the cycle and cause us to abandon our efforts sooner than usual.

The Piedmont of North Carolina is a region where summer storms can mount quickly, and rainfall can entirely pass your garden by. I have often left a torrential downpour in Pittsboro, delighted to think of the wonderful drink provided to the orchard, only to find the rain squall passed my house entirely.

The dust on my parched lane is a horrible harbinger of missed storms gone by.

Early in the summer I pull water from the fish pond by the bucket full and deliver it to the peonies, or the crabapple trees or the forsythia, but as the pond level drops, to the point where we start to worry about the survival of the fish, we stop that practice and begin to wonder about other water strategies we might deploy.

Rainwater always jumps to mind, but thus far all of my homemade attempts have failed. I've elevated 55 gallon drums beneath downspouts, which become so filled with mosquitoes that Tami would travel around the house and dump them out.

I once bought a round 500 gallon plastic cistern and plumbed a garden hose attachment to a nipple on the bottom of the unit. I then elevated it on a rectangular metal stand I found down at Summer Shop. I modified my downspouts to direct the water of two roofs its way. I even caulked around the downspouts to keep the mosquitoes out, and for a month or two, I relished my nightly watering that came not from the well but from the sky.

That worked great when there were a couple of hundred gallons on hand, but with a good rain, it filled to three hundred and fifty gallons and at that point the legs on the stand began to sink into the ground, the stand shifted, and pulled away from my eaves. It was a dangerous folly, which I drained, and reset with concrete footers.

When I caught five hundred gallons of water, I was delighted to see that the stand held its position, but as the hot sun of summer pounded down on the tank, the plastic began to warp under the weight of the water, ultimately reshaping the vessel to the point of being useless.

One year I attempted to fashion a rotary gear pump to the stationary exercise bike that Mary was discarding. I figured it would be simple enough. I was going to place the bike on the edge of the pond, and plumb it to an elevated drum in the corner of the garden. I would then add, "filling the drum" to the list of children's chores. I envisioned the day when they wanted to cross the creek to play with a friend, and I would allow it as long as the drum had been filled.

But fastening a pump to a bicycle is not a mean feat, and proved to be a task beyond my fabrication skills. I ended up with a solitary pile of metal scraps — part bicycle and part pump.

Despite the failure, I went on to order a bicycle powered pump kit from Guatemala, and the fabrication of such remains on my life list. As a community we are only beginning to come to terms with drought. Neighboring towns are seeing watering restrictions put into place. Car washes are starting to reuse water. Water recycling systems are starting to attract attention.

As I drive along the edge of Jordan Lake in summer, I first see the mud flat emerge where the water used to be. They are rich in nutrients, and green up very quickly. As the water level in the lake continues to drop, land bridges to the newly green mud flats appear, and shortly after the land bridges appear, the litter of fishermen taints the flats. Abandoned lawn chairs, forsaken tackle, broken Styrofoam coolers which once held beer or bait, and the many containers left behind from so many individual servings of soft drinks, or Gatorade, or beer, are strewn throughout the lake.

It normally only takes a passing hurricane or two to fill the lake back up, but hurricanes tend to come later in the summer, and while their arrival can be terrifying and devastating, the water they bring the region is often greatly appreciated.

Irrigating our crops is something we are learning to do. We are seeing the rise of drip irrigation systems, and soaker hoses buried beneath water retaining mulch. As more of our wells remind us of the falling aquifer beneath us, farmers are increasingly turning to irrigation ponds, running pond water through sand filters to screen out particles that might clog their drip systems.

◇◇◇

Taking our food products to market is not the struggle it once was. We have Eco Organics, a spin off of Carolina Farm Stewardship Association, (CFSA), which operates giant coolers, and distributes organic and sustainably produced food to fancy restaurants and grocery stores throughout the region. They are a co-op, paying annual dividends based on the production of each grower, and as a wholesaler, they can take large quantities of food.

We have burgeoning farmers' markets throughout the region: in Pittsboro, and at Fearrington Village, and in Carrboro, Durham and Raleigh. Piedmont Biofarm ships a thousand dollars a week worth of produce at the Durham Farmer's Market alone.

And we have Chatham Marketplace, which gobbles up as much locally produced food as it can find.

With soil, water, and market in place, our area is well positioned to feed itself in a sustainable way.

Housing Ourselves

Living in the Woods

As long as I have lived in these woods there has been an abandoned logging road that wound its way from Summer Shop to a large trash pile on the property line, crossed a steep slope, and hit a long flat run along the edge of Bowser Branch.

I used to follow it to its "T," knowing that if I headed right I would encounter Tom's domain, which was guarded by a pack of blue tick hounds, the howls of which would shake the woods. Tom is a hermit who lives in a fallen-down homestead on the edge of my neighbor's land. He dumpster dives to feed his pigs, and dogs, and chickens, and himself, and he is an interesting fellow. He's well-read, and an astute thinker, and he prefers his subsistence gig to full engagement with "civil" society.

For awhile Tom and I farmed my place cooperatively, and we have spent several nights drinking together. We parted ways on the matter of digging ferns.

There was a point when Tom would take his shovel and a bucket down to the creek sides and dig young ferns for sale in a plant store in Sanford. I objected to this practice on the basis that it was extractive in nature, and that Tom had no idea what he was harvesting, nor was he doing anything to replenish the ferns he was selling.

As we argued the point, I suggested there were a hundred and fifty varieties of ferns, and perhaps he was fetching fifty cents for the last one on earth.

My position landed me on the "tree hugger" column of Tom's ledger, and the spirited argument brought our drinking engagements with one another to an end. He also stopped digging ferns.

One year my daughter, Jessalyn, transplanted some ferns from the creek to beside the garden gate, and each spring as their fiddleheads emerge I am reminded of both her and my fight with Tom.

Taking a left on the logging road leads to the banks of Stinking Creek, which was posted with signs that read, "No Trespassing by Order of the Apex Hunting Club." I would timidly cross the creek on stepping stones and wander about the hunting club lands, exploring old homesteads, and beaver dams, and makeshift roads which were occasionally lined with cracked corn and always lined with deer stands.

Our place, and the tract of the Apex Hunting Club, were ancestral hunting grounds. My first deer season in my tarpaper shack was a bit like living in Vietnam, with bullets ricocheting off rocks near the front porch.

A common way to hunt deer is from up in the trees. Apparently the deer are not inclined to look up. Which means they fail to notice the fellow in the deer "stand" with the rifle and scope. Each year I would dislodge a deer stand or two, and have several run-ins with those who were accustomed to hunting the place. I used to trade hunting rights for buckskins and freezers full of deer meat, but as we started populating the place with children, I became increasingly restrictive.

With my parcel off limits, the Apex Hunting Club felt the pressure on their side of the creek. Theirs was a limited member organization, in which they passed the hat amongst their own to raise the money to lease and maintain the place. Maintenance was largely focused on aggressive posting of "No Trespassing" signs on the periphery, which is not a trivial undertaking on a large piece of Carolinian forest.

Ours was a cordial relationship. When I found trespassers on my side of Stinking Creek, who would drive to the water's edge, and cross over to hunt, I would politely ask them to leave. And whenever I was caught trespassing on their side of the creek, I would politely ask them not to shoot.

In those days of wandering the woods, learning about the flora and fauna of the place, I was following the real estate development work of Wallace Kaufman, who later went on to pen a marvelous book about Chatham County real estate entitled *Coming Out of the Woods*. Wally was a naturalist, a mushroom hunter, an ecologist, and in his earlier years he wore the mantle of "environmentalist" well. He was plucked from the woods to become an "expert witness" in lawsuits regarding the construction of Jordan Lake, a seven-thousand-acre Army Corps of Engineers flood control project which put most of Chatham's best farmland under water. Wally emerged as an expert because he had "developed" a compact community in the woods called Saralyn.

In a region where soils tend to trap wastewater, rather than letting it "percolate" down to the water table, it can be hard to find a "perc site" suitable to locate a residence — and to do so often takes several acres of land and the digging of many soil samples before health department approval can be granted.

Those with soils which "perc" can sell real estate for residential development. Those with land that doesn't "perc" can lease to hunters.

Wally pioneered the local version of the compact community, laying out ten-acre lots, each with its own well and "perc site," and each with access to a road. He also penned restrictive covenants that were designed as ground rules for the new residents of the community, such that they could live harmoniously with one another.

In a vast rural county where land is often unzoned, and beyond the easy reach of police, and ordinances, covenants in part played the role of "law." Each compact community would form a homeowner's board, which would mediate disputes, and amend the covenants as needed, and collect dues such as those necessary for the maintenance of shared roads.

In my early days of exploring the Apex Hunting Club lands, I began to fantasize about what would be involved in building a compact community. I found myself digging up other people's covenants, and enquiring about the success of neighboring subdivisions. I'd been lucky with real estate investments in the past, and I loved following creek beds and old roads and stomping along abandoned power line cut-throughs.

Our woods regenerate so fast, with blackberries and wild grape, poison ivy and saplings that it is virtually impossible to pass through without the aid of a former clearing. Occasionally I would find a wildlife trail that would make walking possible, but in general I stuck to those that had been previously visited by humans.

As I was wandering and contemplating, a group of friends were forming Blue Heron, a co-housing project on the other side of the county. Barbara and Sally and the founders of Blue Heron were deeply into the "process" side of community development. They held Scott Peck weekend retreats, and delved into one another's past lives, and imposed a therapeutic overlay into their selection of prospective residents. I watched their journey in awe. Part of their strategy was to build a cluster of recycled homes, leaving the lion's share of their acreage untouched by human habitation.

As a Blue Heron ally, I watched my brother Mark go through all the necessary steps to get voted onto their island — and just when they all found him to be a suitable match for their blossoming community, he ducked, bought a house in Moncure, and took a pass on joining altogether.

Mark and I had been in a variety of businesses together for decades, which made it a small step for him to join me in my real estate development fantasy. I envisioned a community along the Wally Kaufman lines, where everyone had ten acres of paradise, and a set of covenants that would permit all to live happily every after.

I dug up the owners of the land leased by the Apex Hunting Club. They were uncertain of how much land they owned. Like much of Chatham County at the time, it had never been surveyed. Land transactions were often settled by the likes of "Grandpa said his part used to go down to the creek."

We had the place surveyed, and found it to be roughly four hundred and fifty acres, including fifty of which they did not know they owned and had subsequently neglected to clear-cut.

Clear cutting ancestral lands is a common tax-paying strategy in these parts. Succession in these woods begins with pines and gum trees, which give way to oak, hickory and other prized hardwoods. Hardwood forest is becoming increasingly hard to find in Chatham County, and our hardwood stands are easy to pass through on foot. They are also sought after by homebuilders, since people prefer to live amongst hardwoods to stands of pine.

I joined forces with Elizabeth, from Heartwood Realty, who was a seasoned veteran of the Wally Kaufman era. She's a wood sprite, much more comfortable finding survey irons in the forest than negotiating pricing at a boardroom table. She digs soil samples, and reads contours and visualizes roadbeds. I spent many a long hour at the kitchen table with Elizabeth formulating our plan.

Her business is in an old house in the heart of town, and she is one of Pittsboro's long-standing pedestrians. Long before they had coined the term "walkable" community, Elizabeth could be seen walking to the Register of Deeds office, or passing the General Store with her dog in tow. When she fills up a filing cabinet full of real estate closings, she's had a good year. A cabinet and a half is even better.

To become real estate developers, Mark and Tami and I formed a corporation named Altadore Investments. Altadore was once a grand estate in our hometown of Woodstock, Ontario. The natural succession for grand estates is often tacky subdivisions, and it was in a largely non-descript subdivision that we grew up. Vestiges of Altadore remained however, including a wrought iron spiked fence that we were required to cross to get to school on time.

I grew up on Altadore Crescent, and would occasionally question my mother about some of the distinctive homes in the neighborhood that were nothing like ours. My mother would say, "Oh, that was the coachman's house," or "That must have been the livery stable."

I would ride my bike around the neighborhood, and repeatedly ask her about the few remaining houses with the unusual architecture.

She would say, "That's Altadore. Those houses were built a long time ago."

We named our development "Abeyance," which means "set aside," and has an archaic French meaning, "to yearn for." We punched in roads, and laid down covenants, and sold lots to friends and neighbors cheap. We buried utilities and dropped culverts in low spots and drove through endless mud showing raw land to all sorts of people.

The overarching goal of our Altadore project was the preservation of green space, with minimal human intrusion — although we could not afford to do a cluster strategy since the entire project was financed by debt and from the moment we closed on a four hundred and fifty acre chunk of land, the race against the interest meter began.

What we envisioned for Abeyance was similar to what we had experienced as children. We wanted to see the woods full of children, who would form into loose packs, and would seek out whatever delights suited their mood that day. They would converge on Cheryl's because she had popsicles, travel to Tami and Lyle's where there was a trampoline, and venture over to Billy and Kathie's to avail themselves of the skateboard ramp in the driveway. That was the vision, and the vestiges of a by-gone era would be the trees.

At the heart of the project was "low cost." We wanted to attract young families. People who were building their first homes. Unlike most covenants, ours had no minimum house size. We were fine with yurts, or cabins. We were more interested in ecological footprint than we were in preserving real estate values.

Traditional covenants tend to work the other way. Banks like to allocate a percentage of their loan to raw land (which they tend to hate since it is harder to sell in the case of foreclosure), and the rest of the loan to the building. Which means that the optimum lending formula is expensive land for a big house. And when you spend a fortune erecting a mansion, you really don't want a yurt going in next door.

We rejected this logic. Although we left singlewide trailers out of the mix, we did allow modular homes. Again, low cost, small footprint was the target. And to the extent that that was the target, it worked like a dream. Abeyance did fill up with young families, who started bearing children, and our vision of a woods full of kids, who could hop on the trails, did come to pass.

Each year Abeyance holds an annual "Trail Crawl," which is a progressive party that travels from house to house through the woods. In the early years Trail Crawl was characterized by three wheeled off-road strollers that could easily cross creeks, and by bags of diapers and baby supplies. Nowadays the children run ahead, devastating the wildlife as they go.

Each year the party shifts locations, with the last residence often spilling late into the night. The organizers shift around from year to year, which makes no two Trail Crawls alike. The year Jan finished her pond; her place was a stop for the party. The year Marshall set up his Airstream trailer and broke ground on his house, he took a shift as host. Revelers meander through the woods, stop at a designated location, dine on the food and partake of the drinks, and then wander to the next place.

It is an event that lets those who are new to this square mile of woods acquaint themselves with the trail network, and meet their neighbors. Most live secluded lives, with twisting driveways that remove their houses from view. Sometimes you can see lights on through the woods on winter nights, but by and large each house is isolated from its neighbors.

The year Maryann and Dean finished their log cabin, they hosted a portion of Trail Crawl. Tina and Hal's has long been a favorite end spot. Their log cabin represents an outpost at the end of the trail network. When they bought the land they were asked if the trail network could extend to their house on the condition that they block hunters from access to the whole.

They agreed to that, and have been trail users ever since.

As the community has grown, outside the borders of Abeyance, the tail network has also grown. When Stacey bought her house, she and I built the Two Pines connector that runs from the Piedmont Biofuels Co-op to our Front Five, which provides easy access to the swimming hole.

Piedmont Biofuels' cooperative fuel-making operation is nestled into the edge of the contiguous woods. Volunteers cleaned up the nightmare mess left behind by the previous owners and converted an abandoned pole barn into their "Wood Management Center." That's a place where they split and store firewood which they sell when the nights get cold. Rachel and I built a connector to the Northwest Passage, which means it is now an easy walk from the Co-op to all of Abeyance.

When the Co-op opened in the neighborhood, it took a shift on Trail Crawl. Oneas and I deep fried a turkey and served it up for weary hikers. That was the beginning of tourism for us. The kids put up a lemonade stand, and we had dozens of party goers pass through the Co-op that year. And there are residents of Abeyance who have subsequently joined the biodiesel co-op and who run on homemade fuel.

As Abeyance filled up with residences, and sold lots to real estate speculators, the land values climbed. Falling debt and increasing land values made for a financially successful project. What looked like a highly leveraged quixotic foray into real estate development at the beginning began to look like visionary genius. At least from an investment perspective.

For the residents of Abeyance, another story has unfolded. My visions of community bliss were quickly dashed on the rocks with the arrival of animals. One owner's unleashed dog became another owner's target of abuse. One person's guinea hens were a neighbor's private hell.

With the coming of humans came the end of tranquility. And the end of gunshots. Hunting season on our bend of the road has become increasingly quieter with each passing year. And darker. Our covenants incorporated cutting edge thinking about light pollution, and the always-on darkness piercing mercury vapor lights that the utility company rents to country dwellers as "trouble lights" were not allowed. Since living in our house we have seen seven such lights vanish over the years, which has literally made our bend of the Moncure road darker and a more pleasant place to enjoy the night sky.

But we did not live at Abeyance, which put us on the other side of the creek from the disputes. Along the way residents forgot about the low-cost lure of Abeyance, and quickly came to long for more expensive roads. Neighbors fought with neighbors, the covenants drew fierce scrutiny, and the community never really emerged as a community at all. Surely there are lasting friendships amongst neighbors, and there may be a general consensus that we are glad to have this residential place for the "quiet enjoyment of nature," but as a study in how humans might live in harmony with one another, and with the planet, I'm afraid it would be best to characterize Abeyance as a flop.

Many residents don't even go on Trail Crawl anymore.

Selling someone ten acres of paradise is a risky proposition. One person's natural area is another person's mess. And for many, covenants are made to be broken. In the early days I tried to explain that a covenant is a promise, and that if everyone agrees to keep his or her promises, harmony would surely come our way. But one person moves to the woods for peace and quiet, the other moves next door to enjoy their off-road motorcycle.

While we successfully avoided the intensive therapeutic process of Blue Heron, Abeyance was way too Jeffersonian in its principles. It attracted rugged individualists, inclined to build their own dwelling in the woods, many with a "get off my property" approach to neighborly living.

Early buyers came for the vision, but as lots changed hands, the vision became further and further removed. In moved crackpots and gun toting survivalists and hardhearted Christians and all manner of folks — all of which had different visions of community, many of which had the start point of "leave me alone."

That is not to say that large "C" community did not take place. We had more than our share of shared meals, and conversations about what Community might look like, but as all the ink dried on all the real estate closings, our big chunk of woods ended up with some sparse friendships, some animosity, and some who are still wallowing in the "vagaries of the covenants" a decade after they were penned.

Sadly, a close inspection of most of our compact communities reveals a similar result. Lawsuits are commonplace. Neighbors can be found feuding with neighbors in Saralyn, and Redbud, and Meadow View and on Eagle's Ridge. Some people fight over who owns the newly discovered spring. Others fight over speed bumps. In one famous case of homeowner disagreement, a resident jacked her car up in such a way that she could floor the gas to get the wheels to spin to grind two grooves in a community speed bump which conformed to the wheel base of her car. Apparently reducing speed was the idea of others in the community — not hers.

If a history of Chatham County compact communities were to be penned, an honest version would include the shooting of other people's pets, the building and breaching of fences, good friends who end up not speaking, arguments over the diameters of fallen trees, and a litany of silliness which is surely unique to our species.

While it could be argued that Abeyance has grappled with less community strife than many other real estate development projects in the county, its residents have participated in mutual struggle and conflict with relish. As has been pointed out many times along the way, as the creator of Abeyance, I don't live in

Abeyance, and the reality is that I moved on to other projects a long time ago.

From an energetic prospective, Abeyance is a colossal failure. There were no energy efficiency measures included in the covenants — as there should have been — and having each lot maintain its own well, its own septic system, and its own driveway is brutally inefficient. I was pleased when Harvey Harman took a copy of the covenants and ratcheted things up a notch by including energy efficiency in the compact communities that he builds.

The one successful energy related covenant, which banned the burning of brush, was largely effective, and in an era before global warming was in the news, when few people gave a second thought to the carbon cycle, the "no burning" promise was ahead of its time. Years after Abeyance was an established community, I was still beating the "no burning" drum which largely fell on the deaf ears of our local politicians.

Feeling the Burn

Down here in Chatham County our air has not yet shifted into what the EPA refers to as "non-attainment."

That's a euphemism for polluted.

From time to time we write grants at Piedmont Biofuels. We've received grants for tanks, and pumps, and fuel dispensers and such.

For the current round of grant funding, Chatham County need not apply. Because we are not polluted enough. That's fine. That means that if we are to receive any grant dollars for now, they can go to our work in Orange, or Durham, or Wake counties.

Before we can qualify for government assistance, Chatham will simply need more drivers, or more smokestacks, both of which we have on order.

Something we are doing in Chatham County, however, is the pointless incineration of any biomass that we don't want to look at. In fall we rake leaves into great piles, and burn them. When we clear for home sites we push the logs and stumps into terrific piles, and burn them.

When the Department of Transportation passes through with a highway-widening project, they do the same thing. I remember crossing Jordan Lake one night when they were working on Highway 64, and entering Chatham was like entering a post apocalyptic science fiction movie, with enormous smoldering piles on both sides of the road.

As I understand it, the carbon atoms found in our vast stores of biomass are destined for the earth's atmosphere anyway. If a tree falls over from old age, all of the carbon it has sequestered will find its way into the food chain, and eventually end up as greenhouse gases, which will then trap the sun's rays, which will lead to things like we enjoy right now: tree frogs singing in January.

Since that is the natural cycle of things, the only thing we can mediate is the rate at which it happens. Which means we are fools to simply burn biomass when it is in the way.

Years ago, in a vain attempt to buffer our family from encroaching bulldozers, my wife and I did a small real estate development. Since it was beyond the laws of the city, we wrote covenants that all the prospective residents allegedly agreed to. One of them was "No open burning." We felt that it was fine to heat with firewood, or to have a campfire for warmth, but to incinerate simply for purposes of removal was idiotic.

We advocated brush piles, which are ideal habitat for wildlife and birds, and we advocated stump dumps, of which there is one on the other side of the road. Our feeling was that we should use those pesky carbon atoms, or at least slow the rate at which they started working against us.

Scientists the world over are scrambling for ways to sequester carbon as a hedge against global warming. Here's an idea: leave the trees.

For the most part the "No burning" covenant has worked fine. Neighbors remind newcomers who never read the rules, and the neighborhood has not been the source of vast amounts of burning.

We have a new slate of County Commissioners here in Chatham. Maybe they will notice that our air is not yet in "non-attainment," and put a stop to ridiculous burning. If they are not going to ban it out right, perhaps they could issue outrageously expensive permits that citizens would have to purchase prior to burning large piles of biomass. If we had people pay for their pollution, perhaps they would search for another approach.

I've spent the last two years building a biodiesel plant on the edge of Pittsboro. Along the way I've pulled handfuls of permits, and been subject to myriad inspections. Anyone interested in increasing his or her intimacy with fire regulators should go build a biodiesel plant. For two years both Chatham County's Fire Marshal, and the NC Department of Insurance have been providing us with fire codes.

I wonder what they would think of an all out ban on open burning. My guess is they would love the idea. After all, they are the ones who deal with the homes that burn to the ground.

But open burning, or its resultant air pollution, are not really regulatory decisions. They are political decisions. We decide whether or not we want to come home to giant smoking piles of debris where the woods once stood.

Maybe we should just keep on burning. That way Chatham can join our neighboring counties in being polluted enough to qualify for some grants.

I've recently become acquainted with Giles Blunden. He's the legendary designer of Arcadia and Pacifica, two co-housing communities in Carrboro. He built sustainability into his thinking, and his designs include passive solar, and active solar, and they are in Carrboro, which is a readily walkable place.

Being with Giles is like sitting at the feet of the master. He's a soft spoken man with two hearing aides who is as happy to reminisce about the community he has developed, as he is to talk about the succession of the woods. He deployed some fascinating financing strategies on his developments, cobbling together an 8 million dollar project with only ten thousand dollars of capital on hand.

One of his many insights is that development of real estate and housing takes time. If he were to embark on another clustered co-housing project, he would like a four year timeline. And he pointed out that people's lives change over the course of four years.

He views the work we did at Abeyance as a suitable paradigm "for the seventies."

The more interesting study in human habitation has accidentally occurred on the edges of Abeyance. When we walk down the old power line, past the swimming hole, we emerge at Joe and Janice's houses. Joe is a stone mason with a bread oven in his yard. Janice is an artist who once shared space with me at

Chessworks. When we cross the creek that borders their place, we step onto Scott and Rachel's back field. When we traverse the field we arrive at the Piedmont Biofuels Co-op, where there is intern housing, and rental residences that are populated by people in the grassroots biodiesel scene.

This is where small quantities of fuel get made. And where there is a sustainable farm — with all the workers associated with it.

And for us, this is where the community is. The trails from our house to these spaces are well-worn. Perhaps it is the swimming, or the Frisbee golf, or perhaps it is the food that comes off the farm. Whatever the reason, it is the area to the left of our house that holds the most vitality and community spirit. This is where trucks and tractors and tools are shared, and where people routinely break bread together. It is a cluster of habitation, with shared wells, and shared driveways, and where energy conservation is at the fore.

It was not intentionally built. Any money that was borrowed was done so by individuals who wanted to live there. Houses are shared, roommates come and go, and the sense of community is palpable.

Despite its flaws, Abeyance did end up satisfying one of its design criteria. It proved to be a durable low-density community in a region where the woods have been marked for deletion. Golf course communities are now in vogue in Chatham County. One developer bought up six thousand acres to build multiple golf course communities.

I once visited his offices in Cary and saw a giant aerial map of the world as he envisioned it. His proposed kingdom stretched from the Moncure Road to Pittsboro, and he bought everything from the wood yard to the lake. Except Abeyance. And our place. And the little community that has sprung up on the edge. Our little square mile of protected real estate was something he simply went around.

Which means that in one sense, Abeyance was a smashing success. In a world that is scheduled to be entirely reshaped by bulldozers, in which briar patches will make way for putting greens and deer trails are scheduled to become fairways, Abeyance will stand. As an oddity.

It could be that some day some kid will ride their bike home, and ask their mother what all those trees are behind the mall. And the mother will say, "That's Abeyance. Those trees were planted a long time ago."

◇◇◇

I sometimes think the success or failure of a community can be measured by its gardens.

Two groups of passionate gardeners ended up in the woods of Chatham County. The first was at my place, where Jenna, Tami, and I enlisted the able assistance of Keith and Tom.

We waded into the woods and cut cedar trees for fence posts — most of them downed by ice storms or previous hurricanes.

We harvested the cedar resource, and built a quarter-acre garden, surrounded by a deer fence that was eight feet high, with proper corners.

The second was at Blue Heron Farm, where a handful of brave souls headed into the woods to form a co-housing community. They harvested their cedar resource, and built a circular garden in the heart of their project, which was about a quarter acre around.

We filled our garden with asparagus and sweet potatoes and herbs and cabbages. We planted corn and amended the soil. Steve and Alisa came out from Durham and planted hops.

And our enormous garden foundered. Jenna moved away and Keith vanished. Tom went back to his shack in the woods. And the garden was left to me. Tim and Kerry jumped in one year, before retreating to their house to do their own splendid garden.

Left to me, the garden was swallowed by weeds and snakes and stinging insects. Paths grew over, the cold-frame lost its paint and rotted, and the asparagus was such a long walk from the house that it always bolted before harvest.

The Blue Heron garden also flopped. No one had the energy to maintain it. When Farmer Doug came to town, it appeared the Blue Heron garden would prosper. He was an expert grower, after all.

But Farmer Doug migrated toward the Community College, and went on to Piedmont Biofarm, where he gained the ancillary support he needed to prosper.

I breeched my fence and put a road through my garden. I then put up a fence to make it a quarter of the size. And when that was too much to manage, I moved the garden into the backyard.

My theory was that if I could see the garden through the window every time I stepped to the sink, I would notice that the asparagus was ready, or that the tomatoes were ripening, or that the morning glories were devouring the melons.

And that worked. My yields increased. I harvest ten times as much produce from a ten square foot garden than we ever fetched from our quarter acre.

Over at Blue Heron the community grew. The garden in the center of the community took years to gain a foothold. It laid fallow some years. It looked neglected. But as more and more people moved onto the land, those with an interest in some garden space put in a row of this or that.

Today their quarter-acre circle is an amazing, prosperous

place. Mowed footpaths of grass lead visitors through rich beds of perennials, and occasionally groups gather with lawn chairs to watch the evening primrose spring into flower — sort of a live version of time-lapsed photography. A stand of corn fills a quarter of the circle, and all manner of produce abounds.

At Blue Heron the garden was built, and waited for the community to come. The community came, noticed the miraculous fenced resource in the middle of things, and went to work. It now has restored gates and a shed for garden tools, and it is a fecund place to wander.

My original garden gate hangs immobile. Deer walk right through.

Occasionally I hire gardeners, and wannabe gardeners, in my undying desire to live amidst an interesting garden. Most of my hiring falls into the category of "make-work" projects in which I am offering "stop-gap" work to itinerant workers.

One fellow was trying to get his new "organic gardener" business launched. With my insatiable appetite for new businesses, I hired him on the spot. He fertilized my wildflower stand. When wildflowers are fertilized, they stop blooming.

I hired one young woman who wanted to garden. She killed the burning bushes I had raised from scratch. Each day when I would return home, I would find more valuable plant material lost by "accident," based on the fact that she didn't know the difference between pacasandra and poison ivy.

I had one gardener who ripped out Arlo's verbena patch. His Ph.D. in agriculture didn't help him distinguish between blackberries and Zafer's raspberries, nor did it keep him from ripping out our oregano.

Surely gardening is a function of editing. When you plant the tall-growing salvias in front of the low growing thyme, it is an error that needs correcting. Yet thus far I have been unable to hire anyone who can successfully edit my garden.

Anyone walking around the Blue Heron garden would be inspired. And the remnants of our garden can occasionally be inspiring.

But I am afraid that I have no hope of competing with the Blue Heron garden. One busy person's effort has no hope, even with hired help, of out performing the garden of a growing community.

Surely those involved in both gardens do not look at the history of each through the lens of competition. No one cares which garden yields more. No one cares which garden is more magical at the firefly time of night.

Yet a massive garden of one is forever doomed. A garden of many has a much higher chance of success.

Fueling Ourselves

The Piedmont Biofuels Story

IN MY FIRST BOOK, *Biodiesel Power*, I chronicled an emerging biodiesel industry, and described our journey from making biodiesel in the backyard to becoming a farm scale operation. The book ended just as we were about to start building a small commercial plant in an abandoned alloys factory.

In the vocabulary of our project, the farm scale operation has become known as the Co-op, and the commercial operation is known as Industrial.

That word probably derived from its original address, which was Industrial Park Drive. But that word also connoted a sense of scale. Piedmont Biofuels Industrial was a big project. Big by our standards, that is — small by comparison to other biodiesel plants.

I started work in a pair of coveralls, and my first job was to figure out how to turn the electricity on in a creepy old industrial park. The four-building compound was on a single meter. Using daylight and a flashlight to find my way, I found the giant breakers which controlled the flow of electricity about the place.

That was in January of 2005. I found a steel rack and a board — a suitable enough desk — which I assembled in the abandoned control room, a place with no daylight and no fresh air. The beauty of the original control room was that it was out of the way — or so I thought — and we were able set up a makeshift office such that we could scrap out the remnants of the alloy business and simply build a million gallon per year biodiesel business.

When you are accustomed to making seventy-gallon batches of fuel at the Co-op, a million gallons feels large. Our intention was to install a two thousand gallon reactor that we could run twice a day. We figured that if we made four thousand gallons each day, and went home for dinner — and if we did that five days a week, we would make twenty thousand gallons per week. We figured that if we worked fifty weeks a year, we would have a million gallon plant.

We designed and built such a beast, which is where we all work today.

And while a million gallons seems like a lot, it is about the amount of diesel fuel North Carolina consumes every six hours.

Along the way we created a rich and powerful website, which is www.biofuels.coop and we buttressed it with Energy Blog which offered occasional insights into our journey. By doing so we ended up having an influence over the North Carolina biodiesel landscape.

It is important to note that we never set out to build a commercial biodiesel facility. At the heart of our project was the idea that individuals could dip their toe into a nearby waste stream — generally used fryer oil from restaurants — and produce their own fuel. To that end we offered classes and workshops and seminars on how to do exactly that, and the Co-op remains a place where individuals gather to share resources to make small quantities of fuel to power their family fleets.

We entered the commercial fray by chance, thanks to the powerful pull of the abandoned alloys plant that had sat in my imagination for years. When I showed it to Rachel and Leif, they were immediately captivated — possibly because the mezzanine was already painted in Piedmont Biofuels yellow and green.

Despite embarking on a commercial project, we continued to push the idea of individual self-reliance and backyard scale. As a result, people started showing up at our door for consultation. Whether it was conversations into the night at the Co-op, or often at my kitchen table, or sometimes at the shared kitchen we built at Industrial — our notion of small-scale biodiesel spread across the state. Today North Carolina has seven biodiesel plants operating — all of them less than ten million gallons — and you will find Piedmont Biofuels' fingerprints on all of them.

In our view one hundred million-gallon plants is infinitely preferable to a single hundred-million-gallon plant. On our project we collect our feedstocks from within one hundred miles of Pittsboro, and we distribute our fuel in the same hundred-mile region.

While other locales are witnessing the construction of hundred-million-gallon plants, which are fed by palm oil from Indonesia, North Carolina's biodiesel industry is currently characterized by small facilities powered by local feedstocks.

Whether it is liquid fuels, or electrical generation, energy is an excellent example of where the human animal has lost its way with regards to sustaining life on this planet. We have spent the last century and a half building giant top-down, oppressive energy infrastructures that require that we move mountains and start wars to maintain. Along the way we have forgotten the simple fact that energy should be generated where it is consumed. The ironic undercurrent of our current energy conversation is that we once had this figured out. These days, Piedmont Bio-fuels receives funding from the Risk Management Agency of the United States Department of Agriculture to assist farmers with making their operations more "energy secure."

There was a time when farms defined energy security. Micro turbines were used to pump water to the herd. Generators were used to power operations. Tractor power was allocated to pumping for irrigation. America's farms were self-reliant and managed their own energy production. By building a vast electrical grid, presumably to give unemployed workers something to do, we flooded the land with cheap electricity that caused farmers to abandon their self-reliant ways.

And now we have the USDA, one of the largest federal agencies, hiring us to help farmers achieve energy security.

We do design and build "farm scale" biodiesel plants, most of which are powered by waste fryer oil which people collect in town. Homemade biodiesel can undoubtedly factor into a farm's energy balance, and the idea of helping people meet his or her own fuel needs remains at the heart of our mission.

$$\diamond\!\!\!\diamond\!\!\!\diamond$$

One of the great unanswered questions in biodiesel is "How many acres would a small farm need to cultivate in order to meet its fuel needs?" We have been curious about this question for five years, and are no closer to having an answer. Implicit in the question is what would the oilseed crop be? Soybeans are the dominant biodiesel crop, and soybeans are a mediocre feedstock for biodiesel. They do not offer remarkable oil per acre, biodiesel made from soy has average cold flow properties, and the emissions profile of biodiesel made from soy lies in the middle of the road.

Sunflowers would be another choice. As would canola. After five years of talking about it, and after spending serious money researching the question, the North Carolina agriculture establishment has some field trials underway.

Also implicit in the question is, "Once the oilseed is harvested, how is it dried and crushed such that its oil can be turned into biodiesel?"

In the past five years we have done a tremendous amount of education and outreach which has by and large demystified biodiesel. We have dragged our mobile processing unit to dozens of venues, we addressed hundreds of audiences, we've lectured at all the neighboring universities, and we have stamped biodiesel firmly into the consciousness of the regional community. But we are not small grain farmers. Small grain farming left Chatham County thirty-five years ago. Which means that in some ways, we are starting from scratch.

We struck a deal with a local developer and are embarking on a bold experiment that we refer to as "Oilseed Community." I outlined this idea in one of my columns in the *Chapel Hill News*:

Building an Oilseed Community

Piedmont Biofuels just signed a lease on 83 acres of arable land that is surrounded by four homes. It was generously granted to us by one of the huge developers who are busy planning a compact community that will be larger than Pittsboro.

They need a few years to plan their development, which gives us a few years to experiment.

Typically, what we do in the Piedmont of North Carolina is build golf-course communities. We do this less because people like to golf than because we need a place to put our wastewater. Over half of the people who live in golf course communities don't golf.

They just want to live in "nature." The human animal
has affection for green space, and for some, that's a fair-
way surrounded by "rough."

This affection means developers can fetch a hand-
some premium by designing their communities around
that which is "green." It can't be just any green, however. It
has to be a "thirsty green." No native species, or drought-
resistant indigenous plants, please. It needs to be a ter-
rain that can take a lot of water.

Wastewater, actually. Water that comes from the new
houses that are built on the green space in the first place.

Because our soils don't typically let wastewater percolate down to the water table, we have figured out that
we can instead use wastewater for irrigation. Bingo. Irrigate a golf course and fetch a premium at the same time,
so that we can build a ton of houses.

My fundamental problem with this scenario is that
I don't golf. And I like my nature a little less manicured.
And I fret about Chatham's vanishing farmland.

At work we use truckloads of oil to make biodiesel.
Some of it is waste fryer oil, which we collect when people
are done frying with it, and some of it is soybean oil from
beans grown in eastern North Carolina and crushed in
Fayetteville. When the weather warms up, some of it will
be liquefied chicken fat. We are not that particular, really.
It's all fat to us. And it all makes good biodiesel, which is
what we do.

Enter the Oilseed Community. It's time to turn the
soil and get a crop into the ground. Sunflowers might be
a good start. Next winter we might give canola a try. It
has more oil per acre than any other crop that can be easily grown in our region. And we would like to use wastewater for irrigation. We believe we can get our wastewater

from the town of Pittsboro, which is wrestling with capacity issues right now.

Our idea is simple. Use wastewater to irrigate crops that we can use for fuel, and let the homes surround farmland instead of golf courses. That way, developers could still fetch their premiums, by offering prospects the chance to live on "green," and have a way to handle wastewater at the same time.

We'll see. The ink on our lease is still drying. We have three years before we are scheduled to be bulldozed. We need to get crops in the ground. We need a wastewater line. And we need to accumulate the knowledge and equipment for small-grain growing and crushing. By the end of our term, we will have demonstrated a viable oilseed community — which developers can look to as an alternative.

Simple. Customers get their thirsty green space that can take wastewater, developers get their premiums, and we get new sources of oil.

The other day I was running this concept past some folks, and it was pointed out that the idea is predicated on new housing developments coming our way. Which is true.

Some would like to stop the earthmovers in their tracks. And there are lots of opinions on how we should cope with our development crush. Some down here want to take a legalistic approach. Some want to take a political approach — packing boards and committees with like-minded individuals.

Others would prefer to isolate us completely. If we blew up the bridges on US 15-501 and US 64 it would certainly make real estate shopping inconvenient. Or perhaps we could try a fence to keep newcomers out.

> I believe that's what we are doing on the Mexico bor-
> der — and they are doing it in Israel right now. A wall
> seemed to work well in Berlin. Maybe we could wall
> ourselves in.
>
> Ours is a cooperative approach. And thankfully, we
> have three years to demonstrate proof of concept.

The fact that we don't know how to plant it, harvest it, dry it, or crush it was conveniently left out of the story. Somehow or another we will figure it out.

And it is important to note that 85 acres would produce a very small quantity of oil. If we used canola, and could fetch a hundred gallons per acre, the 8,500 gallons of resultant oil would be enough to supply our little industrial plant with about a two-day supply of feedstock.

But if we can get proof of concept, if we can take off an oil-seed crop and turn it into biodiesel, the experiment could change the way we develop real estate in the Piedmont of North Carolina. We currently see developments with five-hundred-acre spray fields being proposed and developed. Spray irrigation is one way of disposing of wastewater. If we could get enough of those fields growing oilseed crops, our little plant could sustain itself on feedstocks from the community.

Today we buy virgin soybean oil from soybeans that are grown on North Carolina's coastal plain, shipped to Fayette-ville and crushed into oil. And today we buy chicken fat that starts out on Chatham County farms that feed a chicken kill-ing facility in Siler City. The solid fat is shipped to Fayette-ville and rendered into a liquid form, and sold to us the way we like it. Both scenarios mean we are generating fuel from feed-stocks within our hundred-mile radius, but both are subject to the whims of global commodity markets, which undercut our self-reliance. Today we are working on increasing our ability to collect used vegetable oil from establishments that fry food, and we are working on the oilseed piece to provide us with some feedstock security.

Having a little biodiesel plant on the edge of town can make a great contribution to "hometown security."

I should note that our little project has flopped over its borders some. Chris Jude, our head fuel maker, has opened "Late Shift at the Plant," for which we have built a stage where he books live acts and shows movies. A biodiversity project has moved into the lawn, which means we enter the plant each day through corridors of flowers that are specifically laid out for beneficial insects and pollinators. Sandi has parked a couple of beehives by the gate, Kathie and Billy donated a playground, and Tuesday and I glued up some PVC soccer goals that have given rise to "soccer night."

The plant is routinely a venue for parties. Children swarm to its midst with scooters and skateboards and inline skates, and all manner of wheeled devices. A whole generation will lose their training wheels at Piedmont Biofuels. That is either a reflection of our craving for community, or of the fact that we have a strip of safe pavement.

Tucked into the side of our shared kitchen is a plant wall bio filter, in which volatile organic compounds in office air are drawn through a continuous flow of water to become nutrients for a wall of plants that gives off clean oxygen. It is an indoor air-cleaning device that is based on plants.

And there are projects in the back corners of Industrial that have yet to be brought to life. One of my favorites is a Waukesha generator that we intend to fire on straight vegetable oil. Our idea is to tie it to the grid to sell off the electrons, and to take its waste heat for our biodiesel process.

Having the Waukesha project has helped us reflect on Pittsboro's electricity supply, and has made me reflect on what the world might look like if it were "Pittsboro Unplugged."

My first exposure to local power generation came from Bruce and Dean, both of whom own hydroelectric plants on local rivers.

Bruce had hired on with us to build our biodiesel plant. He was a farmer turned generator repair expert, who could incidentally weld, and fit pipe, and wire pumps, and pour cement, and do about anything else that might be required to convert an abandoned alloys facility into a working biodiesel plant.

But for him that was merely a job.

His real passion is for electricity. He has a little powerhouse on the Deep River that kicks out around 800,000 kilowatt-hours per year. It's tied to the grid, which means his electrons are purchased by the electrical utility, and sent down the wire with all the rest — including those made from coal, or nuclear, or natural gas.

But the electrons are only one part of the electricity generating equation. There are also "green attributes" associated with how the electricity is made. In North Carolina, the big purchaser of green attributes, or "Renewable Energy Credits," (RECS) is NC Green Power.

That's a program that is run by Advanced Energy, a nonprofit, to encourage new sources of renewable energy to join our electrical mix.

In order to provide incentive to new sources of electrical generation, they assembled a pot of money — which comes from voluntary contributions that consumers can make on their electric bill — and distribute that money to renewable electricity generators for their green attributes.

When NC Green Power first came along, the program excited me. And when I went to sign our family up, I was discouraged to learn that our local electric co-op was not participating. To change that, I initiated an email and call-in campaign. I went around the neighborhood, and convinced people to complain that they wanted to sign up to donate to NC Green Power, but could not because our local monopoly was not participating.

In no time at all, our provider changed their mind and allowed us to opt in. At the time my family was consuming about 1000 Kwh per month, and NC Green Power was charging 4.00 for a block of 100 Kwh. In order to offset my family's consumption, I bought 10 blocks, thereby increasing my monthly electric bill by $40.

That $40 was a tax-deductible donation which I viewed as being roughly akin to throwing some money into the collection plate after a rousing church service.

NC Green Power offered different levels of incentives for different types of generation. Electricity made from photovoltaic solar panels was at the top of the list, paying .18 a Kwh. At the bottom of the list was microhydro, paying around a penny and a half. And other sources of generation, like wind, and biomass, and landfill gas, fell in between.

The logic of this is to get the kind of new generation that you want. Clearly NC Green Power wanted everyone to rush out and buy solar panels, so that the price of the gear would fall, so that it would become more affordable, so that more people would do it. And clearly they were not interested in big incentives for hydro.

Most people in these parts hate hydro.

And there can be good rationale for this. Building dams destroys ecosystems. And hydroelectric operations can draw down the water level in a river such that they can create a dry spot, which can also damage the ecosystem. Clearly NC Green Power was not interested in seeing a bunch of folks run out to build more dams to fetch their "green" premiums.

As a donor to NC Green Power, I ignored the logic. I had a 2 Kwh solar array installed in the field in front of my house, and I had it tied to the grid so that I too could become a power producer.

My goal was to make a little more electricity than the family consumed. In order to even get close, by the way, I had to dramatically cut my electricity consumption. I switched lighting over to LEDs, upgraded my appliances, and started beating conservation into the children.

During a typical April the array will dump around 256 Kwh onto the grid. And the family will pull around 236 Kwh back off. This means I have two meters on the side of the house. One is for buying. The other is for selling.

I buy my electricity from Central Electric Membership Corporation for twelve cents per Kwh, and I sell electrons back to them for five point nine cents per kilowatt-hour. I then collect my NC Green Power premium, which is a whopping eighteen cents for my green attributes.

I think it is important to note that tying to the grid is philosophically different than using a solar array to "go off grid." The solar installation community has long appealed to the self-reliant crowd, and the messaging which frequently emanates from that community is underlined by the concept of "When societal collapse comes, I'll be OK. I'm off-grid."

The understanding is that those of us who are dependent on the grid will be in trouble.

But being grid-tied is a different message. For me it suggests that if all of us put a little more into the pot than we take out, we can stave off collapse altogether.

Another argument I like for tying to the grid is that the grid is more efficient than batteries. Off-grid systems are dependent on storing electricity for those occasions when the sun is not shining. Grid-tied systems are only generating electricity

when the sun is shining, but the grid itself has electricity flying
by rain or shine. The losses associated with the grid — it costs
about six percent of the generated electricity to move electrons
from the power plant to your house — are probably equal to or
less than the losses associated with battery replacements and
maintenance.

On my system I did have a small battery bank installed,
which stores enough electricity to power my well. On those occasions when we have ice storms, or hurricanes, and the grid
goes down, our solar system can keep the family in water.

I find that when I can keep the family in water, heating
with the woodstove, we can comfortably manage through any
electrical outage. When we lose water, however, we flee.

It's important to note that electrical consumption is not
the whole picture. We have a stove and a dryer and a hot water
heater that are all powered by propane. Which means we are on
the propane "grid." I sometimes snicker whenever I see "off-grid
self-righteousness" that is backstopped by gasoline generators
or plenty of propane appliances.

And while solar today is an infinitesimally small part of
our electrical generation, it turns out we have significant hydro
resources.

My relationship with small hydro began by merely joking
with Bruce about how much money I was making from the sale
of my green attributes.

Good-natured joking led to a more serious discussion of
why it was he was not selling any RECs. All of the small hydro
operators had colluded on a bid to NC Green Power, and using
the mistaken logic that if "you get all of it, you might as well bid
low," they ended up with their penny and half at about the same
time that their group fell apart, meaning one operator of several
facilities walked off with the whole pot.

Bruce was out of that pot.

In the fall of 2006 I decided to try my hand at selling some of Bruce's RECs. The idea was that he had one turbine turned on, and another right next to it that was idle. I figured that if I could get some money for his production and take that money down to his powerhouse to get the second generator turned on, we would be doing some good for renewable energy in our town.

Trading in renewable energy credits, or green tags, or green attributes, or carbon credits, or whatever you would like to call them is a voluntary market in the United States, which means almost anything goes between buyer and seller. There is one convention in place, which dictates that the REC be generated in the same year that the power is consumed. That is, there is no "banking" of RECs allowed. In non-voluntary markets, such as those countries that have embraced the Kyoto Accord, credits can be banked from year to year.

My journey into the sale of RECs began with the Town of Pittsboro. I asked for all of their electric bills for the year, and did an analysis. In 2005 they consumed about a million kilo-watt-hours worth of electricity. They sent about one hundred and fifty thousand dollars off to Progress Energy, which controls their local monopoly. Not all of that money was spent on electrons. Some was on access charges, and taxes, and three-phase charges, and power pole rentals.

Since Bruce had generated about 800,000 Kwh worth of renewable power, and since he figured he could line up a couple hundred thousand more hours from one of his buddies in the industry, I went to the Town to sell them enough renewable energy credits to offset their consumption.

And in doing so I walked into an eye-opening quagmire, in which no one had the slightest idea of what I was talking about.

In fairness to the Town Board, and Progress Energy, no one was really selling RECs from hydro at the time. All of the big REC deals in the country were coming from wind. But at the

time North Carolina did not have any commercial wind generation in place, and it didn't make any sense to me to have to
line up RECs from far away wind projects, when we had hydro
projects that could get turned on right here at home.

A critical part of the REC market is the chain of trust.
Just because someone has a renewable energy project in place
doesn't mean that the sale of their green attributes entitles them
to a Florida vacation.

The money needs to get plowed back into more renewable
energy; otherwise the purchaser of the RECs is not really putting their money into renewable energy at all.

When I visited Bruce's dam and powerhouse, the idea of
completing the chain of trust became completely clear to me.
When Bruce removes the padlock and slides back the metal
door, you see one whirring turbine pounding electrons onto the
grid. And next to it you see the second turbine, which Bruce
is working on restoring. As he re-wires the generator, he keeps
track of which wire goes where by affixing clothespins to strate-
gically important positions.

My attempt to sell Bruce's RECs crashed on the rocks in
the fall of 2006. I started too late in the year. The Town Board
could not possibly get their heads around the concept in time. I
had quoted them .02 cents per kilowatt-hour, which was asking
them for a twenty thousand dollar investment.

For their twenty thousand bucks they could have been the
first municipality in the state to declare carbon neutrality, and
my guess is that the story would have climbed its way into the
national media.

Randy the Mayor liked the idea, and kept it on the agenda,
but it was way too sophisticated and way too complex to sell in
the few town meetings that remained in the year, and I wanted
to stay inside the "generated in the same year as consumed" convention.

As the calendar approached 2007, we arranged for Bruce to donate the RECs to the zoo, who applied them to the electrical consumption of their veterinary hospital, and to their North Carolina exhibit. Mary Joan, who runs the zoo, was exceedingly helpful in locating 800,000-kilowatt hours of consumption. The zoo, which operates very much like a self-contained small town, burns around 8 million kilowatt hours each year — or eight times as much electricity as the Town of Pittsboro.

The more I learned about the REC trading market, the more fond of hydro I became. I noted to the Town that we have a power plant in the Bynum Mill on the banks of the Haw River that is not operating. It can generate about a half a megawatt of electricity. And we have one in Moncure, on the banks of the Deep River that is not operating. It has a 1.2-megawatt capacity.

The ecological damage posed by these facilities was done generations ago. The dams are in place. The hydro lakes are full of water. The generators are sitting there idle. All that is required is a little investment to get them turned on. And that investment could easily come from the sale of Renewable Energy Credits.

BLAST Internet got their heads around the concept and bought enough Renewable Energy Credits to offset their business for the year.

I'm not sure how much electricity is consumed each year in the Town of Pittsboro. The Town itself uses a million Kwh to pump water and to run its wastewater facility, and to power offices and streetlights etc. The average North Carolinian burns 1000Kwh per month to power their home. Today Pittsboro has a population of around 2500 souls. Assuming their consumption habits are average, that would put the residential population at around 30 million Kwh per year, or 30 megawatts.

Today we have an installed capacity of around 10 megawatts — from Cox Lake to Saxapahaw to Woody Dam to High Falls — much of which is not turned on,

That may seem like a lot of electricity, but it could be generated by a number of distributed assets. At Piedmont Biofuels, thanks to Dean and Bruce, we have a giant generator that we plan to power on vegetable oil. It would kick out almost three quarters of a megawatt, which would be enough electricity to keep the lights on around town. By far the best examination of this subject lies in Armory Lovin's book, *Small is Profitable*, in which he lays out the compelling case as to why we should produce our energy where we consume it.

Without a doubt our largest hydro resource is at the dam of Jordan Lake. When you walk out on the dam of Jordan Lake you can see two things at the same time. The first is the plume of the Shearon Harris Nuclear Plant in the distance, and the other is the tremendous amount of water that is pounding through its spillway. A hydro project on that water could easily generate 30 megawatts, and again, there is no new dam required. Jordan Lake was built to control flooding for the Cape Fear River Basin. Its construction already put most of the best farmland of the New Hope River Valley under water, and took the Cape Fear Shiner to the edge of extinction.

Along the way the Mayor had the brilliant idea of putting turbines at the wastewater discharge of the town. Wastewater, after all, is scheduled to grow over the next decade.

I'm guessing we will see a new hydro project at Jordan Dam, and some wastewater hydro electric generation in the years ahead.

An excellent book for the exploration of this subject is Greg Pahl's *Citizen-Powered Community Handbook; Community Solutions to a Global Crisis*. Like McRobie's *Small is Possible*, it leans toward the "listing" school of literature, but unlike Homer's catalogue of ships, it is a powerful read.

There is no doubt that our little biodiesel plant can make enough fuel to power our community. That part of the equation is solved. Solving the electrical piece requires more work. Turbines would need to be put in place. Existing powerhouses would need to be refurbished. We would need to get our generator running on vegetable oil and sending its electrons into the mix. All possible. All coming soon in the current renewable energy forecast.

⬡⬡⬡

Piedmont Biofuels Industrial is a strange little place on the edge of town that is brimming with ideas, and passionate people who implement them. In the hallway outside the bathroom there is a lending library of energy books. In one office is the Abundance Foundation that is focused on local food and local fuel and renewable energy.

On any given day it is possible to walk away from the constant ring of the phones, walk across a delightful screened in porch, past the life sized chess set in the yard, and through a group of people who have gathered to discuss ways to improve the farmer's market.

Or another group who is designing a vermiculture composting system for the North Carolina legislature. Or a weary fuel maker reading a magazine, with his alarm clock close by his side — alerting him to when the next batch of fuel is finished.

It could be we suffer from short attention spans. Or it could be there is a lot of work to be done. Whatever the case, even the casual visitor will leave Piedmont Biofuels with a sense there is something "different" going on.

Financing Ourselves

THE OTHER DAY I was sitting in Capital Bank in Pittsboro opening a bank account in the name of my son, Arlo. He was a convenient eight years old, which put him ten years away from needing some cash to go to college.

Until today all of Arlo's college savings was tied up in TINA investments. TINA is a Michael Shuman term for "There Is No Alternative." And for those who buy into mutual funds, or who jump into investment vehicles for college tuition, TINA is where their money ends up.

I am a big fan of Shuman's *Small-Mart Revolution*, in which he positions LOIS investments as the opposite of TINA. LOIS stands for "Locally Owned Import Substitution." And Shuman is quite right when he bemoans the few opportunities for LOIS investing.

Arlo knows that Tina and Hal and their girls live at the end of the Northwest Passage — which is a trail he frequents. It leads to his fort. He is a sensitive creature, and gets upset when he hears his father badmouth TINA. I don't think he knows a Lois.

After reading Shuman, I embarked on an economic experiment. I elected to pull ten thousand dollars of Arlo's college money out of TINA stocks, to put it to work in our local economy. Since we have no local credit card companies, and credit card debt is the fastest to flee our town, I thought I could buy up ten thousand dollars worth of credit card debt.

My thinking was that Arlo should fetch a guaranteed 7%. That's a little more than twice what we would fetch if we bought treasury bonds. And it seemed like a reasonable return.

In 2004 Arlo's college fund in TINA dropped a bit. In 2005 it stayed even. And in 2006 it fetched a 12% return.

At the heart of my experiment was the question of which would do better over the decade before he heads for college: a guaranteed 7%, or a bunch of TINA stocks (the management of which is occasionally loaded with fees).

I figured there were two distinct advantages to using Arlo's college money for the experiment. Firstly, Arlo doesn't pay taxes. If he lent out ten thousand dollars of his college fund, and received some interest in exchange, he would stay below the radar of the IRS — just as he was doing when his money was riding on TINA. The poor kid doesn't make enough on his college investments to have to report to Uncle Sam. Keeping taxes out of the equation greatly simplified the experiment in my mind.

Secondly, Arlo is simply a good-looking kid with a big smile and a big heart. I felt that using his college money mitigated risk. Surely it would be more difficult to default on a kid's college fund than it would be to default on his Dad. After all, his father is some cagey old industrialist who is doing science experiments with his children's cash.

And risk is a big issue. The reason TINA portfolios are so popular is that they spread the risk around. The reason debt is packaged and sold is to spread the risk around. Investing in

LOIS takes more guts. Or in the parlance of the investment business, those who tie their money up in local businesses are less risk-averse.

Once I was committed to moving Arlo's money out of TINA, and over to a local debtor, the work began. Finding someone with enough credit card debt was easy. Ten thousand dollars doesn't even dent the credit card debt of most of the people on our project. But as soon as I started working on arranging a seven percent loan for Arlo, I was stopped by a salient risk management factor.

I asked one potential borrower, "What happens if you die?"

"I don't have a life insurance policy."

Which made me envision a horrible car crash in which I would not only lose a beloved fellow worker, but also Arlo's college fund.

There's risk. And then there is risk.

I thought it would be best to loan Arlo's money to someone with a policy. Someone who could sign a note that indicated that their estate could repay upon the event of their death.

It's bad enough to think that the borrower is going to fall in love, and move away, and default on a towheaded boy's college fund. But much worse to think that even those with good intentions could be suddenly killed and unable to cover the loan.

Part of the concept of risk is to spread it over a pool — like a drop of vegetable oil on a rain barrel — which spreads out nicely and restricts oxygen so that mosquito larvae die in the depths. And lending ten grand to a single credit card debtor is a limited pool.

Which left me torn. The low risk was to send Arlo's cash off to a wealth management company, or run it myself with online trading, by which it would ultimately enrich someone in Kuala Lumpur. The high risk approach was to find someone to loan it to in our community.

Enter Diane.

Diane is a master carpenter and cabinet maker of some renown. Her work is exquisite. In an era where wood is comprised of particle board, she still fashions things from cherry. She works with custom home builders, specifying birds-eye maple, and she is the artisan most likely to show up with a load of unbelievably beautiful cabinets made from wood that is stained by the castings of worms.

She is the cabinet maker to the stars, and her work is well known in these woods.

I don't really know Diane that well. We hang on the edges of a similar crowd, but we are not intimate friends. I have been her customer, and she may well have been mine. One time we collaborated as artists together, fashioning a trophy that is still being awarded to choirs about the state. She did the wooden base, Tuesday and I topped it off with a series of stainless steel choir boys. Once her daughter was in the same daycare as my boys, but she was older, and revered, and it would be generous to call them "playmates."

I think of Diane as a brilliant artist, and as a woman of integrity. I would lend her my tools — she has lent tools to me — and I would let her use my shop.

While Diane was married, our family did not hang out with hers. After her marriage ended, we occasionally bumped into her and her new beau at parties — but we never planned to socialize with one another. We did not hang with them as a couple; we had some distance on the whole situation, keeping up mostly through hearsay and neighborhood gossip.

Just as Diane embarked on her new life, she hit a rough patch. Medical problems set in, and in a land without a safety net, she blew her fortune on an operation and medical care.

She moved from house to house, and shop to shop, unable to ply her artisan trade, and she depleted her net worth. You could call her story Medical Hardship 101 — a tale that afflicts the self-employed with fair regularity.

None of which had any bearing on me. When she started working again Tami hired her to do the cabinets in the kitchen at Industrial, and when she was finished, jaws dropped — which is the usual response to her work. She can put a rounded edge where a corner is meant to be, or include some fused glass doors when they are least expected.

From our perspective, we were simply glad to have Diane back. We had largely missed Diane's hardship phase, and we were delighted to have such a talented artist on our project.

The day Diane showed up looking for business advice is the day I had a candidate for Arlo's anti-TINA college fund.

Diane was reconstructing her woodworking business. Able to work again, and feeling good, she had set up a new shop, taken on Emily for help, and was bootstrapping her business with expensive credit card debt.

Bingo.

She had taken her case to local banks. They were uninterested in her ability to restart her business. What they wanted to lend against was her assets. What they failed to account for was that her primary asset was herself.

"I want to get some Worker's Compensation Insurance so I can put Emily on the saw," she said, "but no one wants to lend for that — they just want to be able to seize the saw."

And I knew she was right about that. I thought of Jeff at Chatham Marketplace who once complained about how the notion of "credibility" had been severed from "credit" a long time ago.

I knew Emily. She came to town as an intern for Piedmont Biofuels, and during her semester with us she established her work ethic with ease. She was young, and like most interns, was intent on building skills, and I thought that if Arlo's college fund could help make her an operator of Diane's saw, we would be doing something right in the world.

Diane had credibility with me. So I moved Arlo's money out of TINA, and walked it into Capital Bank. Step one was to create a scenario where Diane could borrow the money from Arlo, and make regular deposits of her interest and principle — just like her monthly credit card payments.

Instead of paying credit card interest rates in the high teens, she was paying 7%. And instead of mailing her money to a far-away bank, she was depositing it into a local boy's college fund.

Capital Bank actually *is* a local bank — although the concept of local banking is infused with considerable struggle.

When Capital Bank opened a branch in Pittsboro, their branch manager came to visit me. That was odd. Normally when bankers visit me it is when they want a signature. So, when Donna showed up my eyes glazed over. At the time I was trying to build a biodiesel plant, and I had little interest in a representative of the status quo with a thick southern accent. In an era when personal sales calls have gone the way of the mood ring, I was slightly impressed by her effort — but I had absolutely no interest in her products or services.

Until she mentioned that Poly owned the bank, and had suggested she stop by to say hello. Poly Cohen is the owner of Lee Iron and Metal — the scrap yard in Sanford where I used to shop during my days as a metal sculptor.

Poly is a good natured and generous fellow with a keen sense of humor. For many years the sign affixed to the chain link fence outside his office read: "Parking for Poly Cohen. All others will be crushed."

I had done many deals with Poly over the years. He sold me scrap metal, I sold metals to him. He connected me with vendors, always being very generous with his Rolodex. The same can be said for his son-in-law, Scot. They had financed projects for me, provided free materials from time to time, and they donated to our local community college when we were trying to get our fledgling biodiesel project off the ground. Toward the end of my time as a sculptor, their family had also become a good customer of my art.

By the time I met Poly, he was a man about town. I believe he belongs to every civic group in Sanford, North Carolina. One day I would bump into him on his way to Rotary. The next he would be coming back from the Elks Club.

I was a little surprised to hear he owned a bank, but it didn't take long to make a whole lot of sense. And I was immediately drawn to moving my business to his bank.

For sixteen years I have banked on the corner of Hillsboro and Salisbury in Pittsboro. It was once Central Carolina Bank, which was owned in Durham, North Carolina. It then became SunTrust, which is owned in Timbuktu. And for all those sixteen years, I have been banking with Virginia, who I have often seen walking to work in the morning.

What is local banking? I went into Capital Bank to discuss moving my account, only to find a woman who doesn't live in Pittsboro. Doesn't know anyone in town. Doesn't know who I am. Which made me pause. Should I move to a stranger who works at Poly's locally owned bank, or stay with Virginia who not only knows me, but knows some of the idiosyncrasies of my banking habits?

Nonetheless, I have slowly started migrating my banking to Capital Bank — and along the way I have been getting to know them better. On one occasion, when I was considering buying the property on the other side of the fence from our biodiesel plant, I said to Richard, the fellow who was selling it, that I would need to get some financing in place to pull it off.

"I know a bank that would like to help you with that," he remarked. It turns out that Richard doesn't just sell real estate — he's also one of the owners of Capital Bank.

Perhaps everyone owns a piece of Capital Bank but me. That's all right. Someone needs to be the customer. Banking with people who know you feels better than banking with strangers.

Something I always found odd about my long-standing relationship with the bank on the corner in Pittsboro is that the credit decisions always seemed to be made from far, far away. The managers who knew me would happily have me submit for loans or lines of credit, or letters of credit, or mortgages, etc., but whether they were approved or not never seemed to be their decision. Small town banks tended to have their decision makers elsewhere, which means their risk profile for me was determined by some formula, or machine, or on some market in a far away place in which my reputation never seemed to factor in.

Poly sent Donna my way because of my reputation. Richard, with whom I had done two different real estate transactions in the past, knew that his bank would be willing to finance a third.

It's good news that we have a local bank. That means we don't need to create one. All we need to do is fill it up with our deposits, and borrow those deposits for our ventures.

I believe that's the way banks were intended to work in the first place.

I do still miss the little bank in Moncure, right next door to Chessworks. It is notorious for getting robbed. The robberies got so bad that the Sheriff's department started parking an empty car in the parking lot. That worked until the local kids started to write "Wash Me" in the pollen on the window shield, at which point the bank started getting robbed again.

In order to secure itself, the bank has installed cameras inside and out, and put a locking door on the front where they will only let you in if they know who you are. And that's only before three o'clock — otherwise you are required to walk through the bullet proof drive-thru window. Someone back at central office must have figured out that "high bank robbery" time of day.

Another thing that is constant about the bank in Moncure is that the manager is merely passing through town on a training shift. None of them lives locally, knows any of their customers, or has the ability to do anything innovative. It is a training branch.

And yet it is not fair to say that anyone with any talent leaves town immediately. In fact, the people who do the work are Sue and Eileen, who have worked there as tellers for many years, and who know all of the local customers. Just like Virginia in Pittsboro, the tellers are the local bankers.

When I call up Eileen from my cell phone, to do some emergency tele-banking because I am on vacation and out of cash — she knows me by the sound of my voice. Rather than requiring secret numbers, or my mother's maiden name, she asks how Zafer is enjoying fourth grade. I can't lie to her, since she gets lots of feedback from her grandson who is in Zafer's class.

But there is a flip side to local banking — whether it is in Pittsboro, or Moncure. All of our tellers are tied to a global economy.

When I receive a Canadian dollar dividend check from the Canadian company where I used to work, they deposit the amount at par value. Which means if the Canadian dollar is worth eighty five cents US, then I am overpaid by fifteen cents on the same day I make the deposit.

Thirty days later I receive a correction notice that says I was overpaid, and my account is adjusted downward by the correct amount.

It's a primitive reflection on a global system. I don't really lean toward the criminal mind, but vast opportunities for abuse of the system do present themselves. No need for guns and stocking caps to loot the treasury of a bank that takes foreign deposits at par.

Whether it is Sue and Eileen in Moncure, or Virginia in Pittsboro, my finances are moving toward Capital Bank, which is truly locally owned.

⬡⬡⬡

I believe the notion of financing ourselves is where we receive the lowest marks as a community — as perhaps it is the most difficult thing to do.

The General Store Café has successfully done it, however, and my hat is off to them. Mimi went into lunches, and Doug Lorie introduced the community to his Green Chili Burrito, and suddenly the property was on the map. Mimi sold it to Richard and Beckett, who sold it to Roya and another group, and it ended up in the hands of Vance and Joyce.

Vance is a master retailer, and he has invigorated the property — managing to grow sales even in the face of Chatham Marketplace's hot bar. From Irish Night to local bands to art shows, Vance and Joyce have managed to pack the place. And when they needed to raise money to buy out the former disgruntled owners, they went to the community for support.

On their first round of financing, many of us bought in with the expectation of little to no return — thinking that merely having the property in our midst was dividend enough. But when they wanted to expand the store, they did it again.

Securities and exchange laws forbid the solicitation of funds from anything other than "accredited investors." That's the government's term for "rich people." If you don't have a high enough net worth, or make a vast amount of money each year, you are not an "accredited investor."

The idea is to protect people from investing their money foolishly. Behind the concept is the idea that if rich people make a rotten investment decision, it will hurt them less than if poorer people do the same thing.

. Which leaves us unable to raise money from people of average net worth. Which leaves us in a lousy position for financing ourselves.

Chatham Marketplace financed their project with low-interest loans from the community, and with co-op memberships, and with a loan from the National Co-op Bank in Washington, DC. Piedmont Biofuels used local money from rich people, as did Shakori Hills.

For the most part, though, we have allowed our financing to go global, which means our debt and our premiums are traded half way around the world, and we have largely lost our ability to influence them.

When Chatham County passes a bond issue at the ballot box — for instance, to raise three million dollars to build a new library down at Central Carolina Community College, they issue the debt to the brokerage community, and it leaves town immediately. I once decided that I would like to buy some of our County's debt, and went about asking how to do it. The president of the College didn't know. Neither did The Friends of the Library. Vicki McConnell knew how to do it — she's an assistant County Manager in Finance — and she issues blocks exclusively to brokers.

In the end I did learn how to buy some of the County's debt. If you would like to do so, call Merrill Lynch. They don't have an office in town, but I am sure they would be happy to help.

⬡⬡⬡

Distinct from local finance, but critical to our local economy is monetary circulation, and in that role we have a local currency called the Plenty. It is one of the most beautiful banknotes imaginable. So beautiful, in fact, that people pin them up on their walls, instead of spending them, which would be preferable.

On the bottom of the bill is the slogan "In each other we trust," which is an apt description, since it is trust which backstops both the Plenty and US currency.

Often when I am introducing the notion of a local currency to a new user, they assume that "real" money is somehow backed up by the bank. Or by Uncle Sam. The reality is that the currency of the United States has not been backed by gold, or silver, or anything other than trust since 1933. The same is true of the Plenty, which has been backed by trust and circulating since 2004.

In the early days of biofuels, our backyard project was a magnet for the insanely self-reliant. We had preachers, and survivalists, and the most rugged of the rugged individualists showing up at our doorstep on a quest to make their own fuel. Most of them wanted to hide from the government, and saw homemade fuel as a way of dodging road taxes.

And many were experts on the history of the currency of the realm. Most would never offer up their "government" names, since anyone using a social security number was not "free." It made it difficult to enroll them down at the Central Carolina Community College, where we were teaching a biofuels course. Some of them wanted to pay their tuition with "constitution silver," and had actual minted coins that they used as legal tender.

Whether it is the Plenty, constitution silver, or the US dollar, the concept is the same. What gives currency its value is how much you can buy with it. If the farmer at the farmer's market is selling garlic for two dollars and fifty cents a pound, and will accept Plenties, than a quarter plenty buys the garlic, and it is the garlic, not the currency that holds the value.

The reason the farmer accepts the Plenty is because he or she knows somewhere where it can be spent. They know that they can take it to their massage therapist, who accepts Plenties, and use them to pay for the service.

And the massage therapist accepts them because they can be used to pay for groceries at the co-op grocery store. And around and around it goes.

Economists refer to the number of times a dollar (or Plenty) goes around as "circulation." They use a "multiplier," to count how one transaction begets another that begets another, and the number of transactions can be used as an indication of an economy's health. When I moved to Chatham County in 1990, our Economic Development Corporation, which is a non-profit funded by our County Government, felt that we had a circulatory number of seven. That is, every dollar spent in Chatham passed around seven times before leaving town. Today Chatham County quotes a multiplier of two. Over the past seventeen years, the big box stores have edged their way into Chatham County, and the decline in our monetary circulation is a reflection of their presence here, and the clear sign of a weakening local economy.

The master of multiplier analysis is Michael Shuman, author of *Small-Mart Revolution*, and many other books on local economy. Shuman likes to use the example of a locally owned bookstore vs. a chain. When we buy books at chain stores, the money is sent to head office immediately. Head office pays the accountants, and writes the advertising copy, and maintains the website, and does all of the ancillary transactions necessary to sell that book. A local bookseller, however, hires a local accountant, buys advertisements in local media, and hires the local web provider to maintain their website. Which means that dollars which are spent locally, circulate more readily, and more circulation is a sign of health.

At the heart of the concept of a local currency is the idea that only local merchants will trade products and services for Plenties, which means the circulation has to remain local. That is, unless you encounter a Plenty, and think it is so beautiful that you decide to hang it on your wall instead of spend it.

The Plenty intentionally limited its circulation area to a narrow swath from Hillsborough to Pittsboro, accepting Moncure Chessworks at the end of its southern range. The intention is to not be distributed across the Triangle, but instead to keep the circulation in a relatively tightly defined geographic range.

The masterminds behind the Plenty were Matt and Clarissa, and a handful of friends gathered around a kitchen table in Carrboro. They have day jobs as technical people in Research Triangle Park, or as mothers, or artists. Some work full-time at nonprofits.

Ideas are always easier than implementation, but the Plenty made it out of the ideation stage into reality, and was widely accepted by artisans, trades people, and sole proprietorships of all types. Those wishing to become a "member," send in fifteen dollars, and receive five Plenties in return. Apart from being an excellent return on investment right off the mark, membership came with the inclusion in both a print and an online directory.

Those who embraced the concept of the new local currency altered their buying habits. Our biodiesel co-op became a member quickly, and when we needed to rewire our physical plant at the donated double-wide trailer which was our new location, we looked to the Plenty directory, and found Deb, an electrician who accepted partial payment in Plenties.

One aspect of accepting payment in Plenties is that each member could specify the percentage of each transaction they would allow. That is, if Deb accepted ten percent payment in Plenties, and did a thousand dollars worth of wiring work, we were allowed to pay her nine hundred dollars plus ten Plenties. And so the circulation begins. She picks up a new customer because of her involvement with the local currency, and we are assured of spending our money locally.

One of the criticisms of the Plenty is that the local trades people are going to spend their money locally anyway — and do not represent the big "leaks" in our economy that the Plenty is designed to plug. But artisans spend money too, and they need groceries, and goods and services like everybody else.

An early anchor of the currency was Weaver St. Market, a co-op grocery store in Carrboro. They put a Plenty acceptance policy in place, and started offering the Plenty as change. Shortly after that, Vance at the General Store Café started accepting Plenties in Pittsboro, and after that came BLAST Internet, and Edwards Antiques, and French Connections. Suddenly it was possible to pay for your lunch, your fuel, and your monthly Internet service all with the local currency.

Lunch dollars probably stick around longer than most. Local proprietors consume local services, and it's not until they buy their food off the Sysco truck that their dollars leave the community.

Fuel dollars, on the other hand, tend to leave town quickly. North Carolina has no petroleum refining capacity, which means every dollar spent on petroleum goes first to the Gulf Coast of Louisiana, which has two pipelines connecting our state, and then off to faraway lands like Venezuela or Saudi Arabia.

The money we spend on Internet access also tends to leave town immediately. Sprint, (now Embarq) headquartered in Kansas City, Earthlink out of Atlanta, TimeWarner out of Chicago, and BLAST out of Pittsboro, service our region.

I used to be routinely telemarketed by well-meaning contractors for Sprint.

They would begin each call with "Hello, I'm calling from Sprint, your local telephone provider."

To which I would reply, "No you're not."

Which would cause the conversation to pause.

"You're not local. Where are you calling from?"

Occasionally it was Corvallis, Oregon, or Lubbock, Texas, or any number of distant cities.

Sometimes they would concede that while they were not physically "local," they were the "local telephone carrier."

Which would lead me to ask, "Do you know where Moncure is? I noticed the other day when I tried to order a new phone line for our co-op, your company told me they did not service our area. Which I found funny, since I have three other phone services in the neighborhood, and your company is my only choice."

Some telemarketers relished the chance to spar with me on this topic, and we would explore the subject at length. Some would put me down as an "alertable" nutcase and try to escape the conversation. And some would get their supervisor to call me right back.

Whenever my children would overhear these conversations they would tend to be embarrassed on behalf of children everywhere. They are much happier to see me write a book about local economy than to explore the subject with random strangers who were calling during our dinner hour.

❖

The trick to a local currency is circulation. And circulation is based on where you can blow banknotes. Any time circulation stops, the whole project is diminished, and unfortunately, the flow of the Plenty stops from time to time.

One time Moncure Chessworks sold a patio sized chess set to the General Store Café, and accepted 100% payment in

Plenties. It was an enormous wad. Vance was delighted to shed his Plenties, since he had been hoarding them instead of circulating them. Chessworks got them back into circulation by buying many lunches, and paying artists, and blowing them wherever they could.

When I was at the helm of BLAST we accepted them at par value. People on dialup access mailed in a couple of Plenties a month. It was quaint. And fun. And I signed up a bunch of employees who would accept one Plenty a month in their pay.

BLAST has long paid its employees via direct deposit, an electronic transaction that has undermined the meaning of "payday." Money just hits the account. No need to have contact with your supervisor. No need to go down to "payroll" for your check. The bank account just swells automatically.

Our payroll service would generate a little pay stub that would show withholdings for Social Security, and deposits into savings plans, and taxes set aside, and I noticed the pay stubs would frequently end up in the recycling without getting opened. Getting a pay stub is not like getting a paycheck.

So I started writing notes on the pay stubs. I would say things like, "Tarus, nice work this month, congratulations on getting the Harvard Medical School deal."

Or I would write, "Laura, you are an amazing, powerful person, and I am glad you are here."

And I noticed that when I wrote notes on the bottoms of the stubs, they started leaving the building with the employees.

Those who signed up to receive Plenties as pay, started looking forward to their envelopes, since throwing them away was like throwing away a ten dollar bill.

BLAST had Plenties coming in the mail, and going out in pay, and whenever they started to pile up, I would walk around the office and give them away.

When Chatham Marketplace opened up, it accepted

Plenties from the get go, but I'm not sure they got the circulation piece. Instead of using Plenties to pay their BLAST bill,
and their employees — some of which drive around on biodiesel — they tended to squirrel them away.

Which means the number of Plenties in circulation is not
equal to the number that have been minted, which means their
value proposition is in peril. We need all the Plenty dams to
break in order for true circulation to begin.

Geographical Discrimination

On one occasion when I handed one of our designers a
Plenty, he eyed it carefully. "What's this?" he said.

"That's lunch at the General Store," was my reply.

When he came back with, "What is the General
Store?" I was stunned. My disbursement of Plenties re-
vealed an enormous ignorance of our local economy. I
had people on staff that woke up on the other side of
Jordan Lake, and commuted for an hour across the Triangle, entering Pittsboro from the eastern side of town.
They would past the Post Office, come to work all day,
and leave by the same route. They had never made it
into town as far as the roundabout, which encircles the
courthouse, upon which the General Store is nicely
located.

That incident led me to believe that it would be best
if we rid ourselves of all commuters. Commuting is the
death of community. Most of the people of Chatham
County wake up when it is dark and leave town to their
faraway jobs. I figured it made no sense at all to employ anyone who did not live locally. By the end of my
watch as CEO I had successfully applied "geographical

discrimination" to the point where I had rid the firm of almost all of its commuters.

And before the sheriff starts driving down my lane to serve papers from all the former employees who now feel like the victims of geographical discrimination, I should point out that it is completely legal.

If you want to serve on the Raleigh police force, you will live within a certain distance of the police station. The same is true for firefighters. All government agencies should employ such a policy. That would keep us from hiring tourism directors who don't live in our midst, or economic developers who drive into our county seat to work every day, and leave town every night. People who live in a community have a vested interest in strengthening that community. Those are the ones who accept and receive local currency. People who live far away take their expertise, and their spending power, home with them each night. They have no interest in a local currency, which is specifically geographically limited.

Who knows? Perhaps it is just as important to have people circulating amongst ourselves, as it is to have currency circulation. Perhaps savvy economists in the future will figure out a way to measure the impact of a population that lives locally, and assign a "multiplier" to that. There is the very real possibility that when we fall into measuring our economic health by mere currency we are missing the point entirely. There is wealth, which we can easily count by who has the most money in hand. And there is standard of living, which is another thing entirely.

The meditative value of riding a bike to work, or

the fitness value of walking to lunch, is not included in the proposition of either the US dollar, or in Constitution silver, or in the Plenty. It could be that currency is a rotten measure of things in and of itself.

And while we are at it, we need the currency to "cross over" from the alternative folks to the mainstream. Just like a country and western song can occasionally cross over from the country charts into the pop charts, the goal of every local currency should be to hit the mainstream.

One of the things that plagues the Plenty is that it has never managed to do that. It is still firmly entrenched in the "alternative" world. Perhaps this is because its users don't belong to Rotary, or perhaps it is because they have excluded "real" business people from their board of directors, or perhaps it is because the good folks who started — and drive — the Plenty are not business-oriented. I have met with them a number of times, and whenever I do I make the claim, "You need a bank." If they could get a local bank to accept Plenties, a large amount of fear and uncertainty would melt away. More users would sign on, and more firms would accept the currency as tender. Furthermore, a bank that accepts Plenties would suddenly be forced to have a toe in the local economy. Banks pay for services like any other business. They could spend Plenties too.

When I was at the Green Festival in Washington, DC, I had the pleasure of being in the audience for a Michael Shuman talk. One of the audience members asked his opinion of local currency. He stated a preference for local credit cards instead. It is easier to get broad-based acceptance of a local credit card, and it keeps the convenience up.

Another time, when I was in the audience of a presentation at the Sustainable Biodiesel Summit in San Antonio, one of the audience members alluded to the fact that the E. F. Schumacher Society has a local currency in play in New England. Ithaca, New York, has a famous local currency that has been studied by academics. Their conclusion is that the region of the local currency has seen an increase in the standard of living since its introduction.

It's hard to make a similar claim when it comes to big-box shopping infrastructure. When we spend a dollar at Wal-Mart, it is counted once in Siler City, shipped off to Arkansas to be counted again, at which point it immediately leaves the country. I am uncertain as to whether or not the presence of a Wal-Mart in our county has increased our standard of living. It could be that all of those "Everyday Savings" diminish us in multiple ways. It could be that we should get our local Wal-Mart accepting Plenties. That way the users of Plenties could get the benefit of trapping their money in a local economy, and the benefit of Wal-Mart at the same time.

Although the Plenty is a fledgling currency, and although overall we tend to do a rotten job of financing ourselves, it is an area that would rapidly recover were an economic shock to occur. We are a trading species, and despite the fact that we have created complex systems of finance that are far removed from our local economy, it is an area which would immediately recover.

After all, trade is based on "things," not money, and as long as we can create things, like food, or fuel — or as long as we can offer services of value — like massage or art, our self reliance will be readily apparent. In the end trade is a function of trust, and it is trusting one another that lies at the heart of our local economy.

Educating Ourselves

The Education Pie

ONE OF THE VERY strange things about education in the US is that it is competitive. Our project, Piedmont Biofuels, largely arose from the Community College in Pittsboro. That is where we came from, and that is where we continue to teach.

Back before there was such a thing as global warming, Rachel and I were down at Central Carolina Community College (CCCC), teaching "Energy Class." Someone from our project has taught biofuels there for the past five years. To say we are enmeshed with CCCC is an understatement. Leif and Rachel still spend time on curriculum development, Evan and David both teach, and Andy is employed full-time by the college to get the word out on both green building and biofuels. He's one of us. He comes to our staff meetings to provide us with updates from the perspective of the College.

And Farmer Doug is one of us. He left the land lab down at CCCC to open Piedmont Biofarm, which has become an active player in our local foodshed.

We can view our relationship to the college a number of ways. We can break their hearts when we steal their best employees — like Rachel and Doug. Or we can call it "technology transfer," in which their brainpower is leaving the academy to fuel private enterprise.

Our start point is that we get everything we want or something better — there is nothing better than Rachel or Doug. Thank you, CCCC.

And CCCC gets everything it wants. Since Rachel left their employ, she has clubbed tens of thousands of dollars worth of grants for their analytics program. And she landed enough cash to pay for a full-time position for Andy, who helped formalize the biofuels curriculum so that it could go statewide. And we are delighted to give CCCC credit for their role in our success along the way.

Which means they attract students. Which means they get funding from the state, which means we are simply good for the college. And the college is good for us. I explored this concept in a piece I wrote for the *Chatham County Line:*

Our College Canvas

Down on the edge of Pittsboro sit the red brick buildings of Central Carolina Community College (CCCC), which is an institution that we can view a couple of ways.

For many educated folk the state's Community College system is a "second string" academy. Here in the shadows of UNC, Duke, NC State, Meredith, Elon et al, it is a place for the poor performers. It is often viewed as the Junior Varsity of educational institutions.

This view is sometimes reinforced by those employed by the Community College System. It is, after all, encumbered by state mandates, which include everything from low pay, to teaching contracts that do not include benefits, to a bureaucratic demeanor.

It's easy to throw darts at the college.

But there is another way to view our college. It can be viewed as a canvas, on which we get to paint our ideas.

One of the great painters of our Pittsboro college canvas was Harvey Harman, who introduced the Sustainable Agriculture Program. Harvey is the proprietor of Sustenance Farm, and one of the results of his work at the college is a growth in the number of farms in Chatham County.

Surely we need to credit a whole bunch of people for the success of the Sustainable Agriculture Program at CCCC. What started as a vision became a land lab, complete with a Community Supported Agriculture (CSA) program, a working farm, and a curriculum that has become renowned on the Eastern Seaboard.

In an era of vanishing farmland, where local foodsheds are embattled by encroaching golf courses, our college is inspiring people to go into sustainable farming.

Thank you CCCC. Its administration, its staff, and the institution itself helped enable a remarkable program.

The same thing happened with the Biofuels Program. Rachel Burton was innocently running the Automotive Program at the college, when she invited Leif Forer to jump in, since he shared her passion for biofuels. Together they built a program that not only endures, but also draws students from all over the country. The curriculum developed by Rachel and Leif is now freely available to the academic community. It has been replicated in Alamance County, and is sought after by instructors nationwide. The next introductory Biofuels course starts on August 24th.

One of the offspring of our community college is Piedmont Biofuels, which has accidentally become an award-winning national leader in sustainable biodiesel production.

In many ways the relationship between Central Carolina Community College and Piedmont Biofuels is exactly the relationship envisioned by the founders of the Research Triangle Park. One of the ideas behind the park is that the academy would spawn industry, and industries would in turn hire graduates of the academy.

Bingo. CCCC just received a big chunk of funding from the NC Legislature, thanks in part to Senator Bob Atwater and Representative Joe Hackney, and the college is currently bringing a Biodiesel Analytics Program online under the auspices of a Biotechnology Program. It's no surprise that Piedmont Biofuels, and another dozen biodiesel projects across the state, are in need of lab skills from people who are intimate with the biodiesel specification and the properties of the new fuel.

As a canvas, CCCC is designed to create jobs for the people of North Carolina. It allowed Rachel and Leif to paint the broad strokes, and it is filling in the colors of a masterpiece underneath.

Classes at the college are only the beginning of the educational piece. They also host workshops, and conferences, and from Piedmont Biofuel's perspective, the outreach and education never ends, including free tours of the Moncure Co-op every Sunday afternoon — an event that brings thousands of visitors to Chatham County.

What is next on the easel? Green building is gaining speed. Alicia Ravetto and Paul Konove, along with Harvey Harman and a cast of others are working on a

Certificate Program in green building. Not a bad idea for a town of 2500 which has 10, 000 building permits issued.

Our college canvas sits on the edge of town inviting our ideas, and our talent, and it assists us in creating our community and our economy into whatever it is we want them to be.

Did I hear something about an arts incubator in Siler City? Was that a cooking school I heard rumors about? Film making, anybody?

In a culture that is quick to enumerate our problems, perhaps we should consider counting our assets, and when we start doing that, let's put our Community College on the top of our list.

Something in the human animal prefers to look at the size of its own slice and ignore the size of the pie. Educational institutions are trained to vie for students. With a deep tap root into scarcity, the community college system feels it is competing with the land grant universities, which are competing with the other universities, which are competing against the private schools.

It is as if there is only one student shopping for a class.

Which might be true when the institution is entrenched in teaching business as usual. I suppose that demographically speaking, the cards are stacked against the schools. Schools may be slotted to simply get smaller as our population bubble moves out of the education time of life and heads for the old folks home.

Which is a funny thing. Education is something the United States used to export to the rest of the world. Since it is not included in the balance of trade numbers, it gets forgotten. In the global economy the balance of trade is measured in widgets and currencies. When the Chinese take our currency and our promises to pay and ship us lots of widgets, we appear to have a vast deficit in our balance of trade with China.

Yet where would the Chinese go if they wanted to study something like, say, physics?

The answer is they would line up at the best schools on the planet, and a whole lot of them are in the US.

Maybe it was 9/11, or maybe it was Homeland Security, or maybe it was the Bush Administrations, but something truncated the flow of education from America to the rest of the world. Student visas dried up and the importation of foreign interns became a nightmare.

One time a fellow in touch with the Gates Foundation who was looking for ways to fund technology transfer to the developing world contacted me. I have long held that if anyone is interested in helping the developing world, they should send their aid to Chatham County, North Carolina. But I didn't think they would find that amusing so I told them they should figure out a way to let interns back into the country so that they could learn things in America that they could take back to their native lands.

Part of me thinks that if we are no longer able to ship widgets (or resources for that matter), we might as well ship education. And another part of me is delighted by our new inward focus. When we teach sustainable agriculture here, it means I will have something to eat. When we teach it to refugee farmers from the Sudan, it means they will go home and figure out how to feed people, which is not nearly as helpful for my personal survival...unless I am selling them the education to begin with.

America has become reclusive since 9/11. A friend of mine, Kirsten, arranged to study abroad in Ecuador. She is an exceptionally bright kid who began her studies in veterinary medicine and biological sciences. As she progressed in her studies she began to focus on the spread of diseases — specifically those which jump from animal to human populations. Before leaving the country to study abroad she received a wonderful scholarship from Homeland Security. Apparently disease expertise is on their list. It was nice to see that her cash problems were behind her and that her education was financially assured. But there was a catch. If she was to take the Homeland Security offer, she would not be allowed to leave the country. Goodbye Ecuador.

If we close our doors to visiting scholars and interns, and we cloister our greatest minds inside this country, then our ideas of sustainability will not make it to the rest of the world. I like Karl-Henrick Robert's vision, which dictates that sustainability must be global in nature in order for it to work. He's the creator of the Natural Step, a visionary program out of Sweden.

I wonder about the irony of suggesting our ideas must circulate globally in a book about local economy, and suspect that education is something that needs to be global. It strikes me that a much better defense against future 9/11 events would be to raise the education level of everyone on earth.

⬡⬡⬡

At one point Piedmont Biofuels decided to hire a full-time Education Director, and to do so we ran the advertisement nationwide. This is when we learned about that mythical lone student.

First contact came from Solar Energy International (SEI) in Carbondale, Colorado. Rachel and I have both taught there, and they have used Piedmont Biofuels as their "biodiesel arm." They are a scrappy institution that arose when Johnny Weiss left the local community college system to teach renewable energy thirty years ago.

And after slogging through the decades, they have landed on their feet with an excellent reputation, a worldwide following and a business that runs about a million dollars worth of training a year.

Anyone looking for a delightful week away from his or her daily grind should book a course on photovoltaic electricity production at SEI. Carbondale is an amazing walkable community, the place is packed with passionate instructors and dripping with innovation, and grassroots drive. One of their main buildings is shared with a community radio station, where they frequently hold legendary "end of class" parties.

We love SEI. When we posted our ad for an Educational Director, we felt like we were taking the first steps toward becoming SEI. Our idea was to consolidate all of the education and outreach activities in which we were involved. At the time, Rachel was developing a curriculum at Industrial, for use by the National Center for Appropriate Technology. Matt was leading Clean Technology workshops with our mobile biodiesel processor from the Co-op, and I was teaching a class at NC State. Our efforts were scattered. And we thought we could focus them, and increase them, by simply adding a person who could assume responsibility for the whole.

Which worried SEI. They didn't want to lose their biodiesel arm. Which led to long conversations into the night with the folks from SEI, convincing them that we were not trying to "compete," or steal students. We were focused on the size of the pie.

In the case of biodiesel, the industry measures itself by the gallon. Its petroleum counterpart measures itself by the barrel. There are forty-two gallons to the barrel. Which means biodiesel is infinitesimal when looked at through the shadow of petroleum.

Next thing I knew the president of the Community College System was sitting on the porch outside the control room where I work. He had seen the ad. And he felt perhaps we were pulling out of the Community College, where Evan and David were teaching a sixteen-week biofuels course, which is required for our interns. It's where Rachel teaches a new class on biodiesel analytics with the lab gear that she managed to get funded by the people at the NC Bio Network.

And so I explained to Dr. Garret that we had no intention of leaving, and that we simply needed to drive our efforts up a notch, and again the same logic applied.

He has a fledgling Green Building Program that is being launched.

It would appear there is ample room for us, and the college to start educating people on green building. Green building is to the status quo home building industry what biodiesel is to petroleum. Time to get started.

And I had a similar experience over at the North Carolina Solar Center. Its director, Steve Kalland, is a savvy operator who has been in the renewable energy space for decades and has shepherded me through many policy tangles.

I often use the analogy of the cat that climbs to the top of a tree, gets scared, and is unable to get down on its own. When I joked with Steve that there was no need for him to be up in a tree, and that I was tired of having to call the volunteer fire department to help get everyone out of the tree, he replied, "I'm not up in a tree. I'm merely standing at the bottom and thinking about heading up."

For years Leif, or Rachel, or I have participated as instructors for his Renewable Energy Diploma Series. His feeling was that if we were going to enter the education fray in earnest, not merely as subcontractors for him, then he might as well cancel the program.

My feeling was that we can run biodiesel courses, he can run biodiesel courses, the college can run biodiesel courses, SEI can run biodiesel courses, and we won't even begin to reach the myriads of people who have heard about biodiesel and are curious.

I invited him to not climb to the top of the tree, and instead to join us in trying to spread the word.

So, Steve is in, although he is suspicious. He has a keen sense of cooperation, and competition makes him wary. When he took over the reigns at the Solar Center, he was careful not to apply to the same funding sources that were propping up Ivan Urlab over at the North Carolina Sustainable Energy Association. By consciously steering clear of the foundations and funders that Ivan depends on to run his operation, the two organizations can peacefully coexist in the same space.

And Steve gets it. He works tirelessly on renewable energy. One time he picked me up at the plant and drove me to Winston-Salem. It turned out the two of us were on the same stage, addressing the Chamber of Commerce, so we carpooled.

One of the things that struck me was that Steve took a cell phone call on our way home. Dr. Hobbs was touching base on some calendar issues for the next day. Two state employees. Working into the night to move the message along. I was impressed.

In terms of the possible, I have utter confidence in our ability to educate ourselves, and I am not worried that the efforts of one group will diminish the efforts of another. Humans can compete. And we can cooperate.

One of the people who understood this instantly was Alicia Ravetto, the famous daylighting architect who has started offering her own series of courses on green building. One day I bumped into her on the porch of the Chatham Marketplace. It was a gorgeous spring day, I had the top down on Creampuff, my Mercedes convertible in which Dias installed a biodiesel engine, and Alicia jumped in for a quick spin to the Co-op. I showed her the building we had acquired next to the Co-op, and explained how we had posted an advertisement for an Education Director and how I wanted her to teach as part of the nascent program we were developing. I was all ready to bring out my "size of the pie" analogy.

But she saw no conflict. And in her thick Argentinean accent she said, "You are grassroots. Your students will get dirty. I am builders. No problem."

It was nice not having to fetch Alicia from a treetop.

Entertaining Ourselves

Entertain Me

ONCE WHEN MY ENTRIES to Energy Blog were flagging, Girl Mark sent me an email which read "entertain me."

I suppose that as a blogger I have furnished some entertainment to those in grassroots biodiesel, though I'm not sure I have tried on the self image of "entertainer."

Yet entertainment is at the core of community.

When you are riding across the rolling meadows of Henderson-Tanyard, just past Bobcat Point, you see a modest sign for Shakori Hills. What was once cardboard and magic marker is now cedar and permanently in place.

The story of the Shakori Hills Festival of Music and Dance is complicated and convoluted and fraught with intrigue — but the background scenes and history are not nearly as compelling as what the visitor encounters by attending year after year.

What was once mud is now a mulched path. What was once a sea of poison ivy is now a garden of Cairns. Today there is a ticket booth, and a parking lot on a fallow field. What was once a derelict farm is now a full fledged festival grounds. Twice a year the gates are thrown open and the place runs wild with children, and hippies, and artists, and music lovers, and carom players, country singers, rock'n'rollers, gospel bands, zydeco players and renewable energy fanatics.

Some come to clog, some come to play chess, some come to try the climbing wall, some come for the alligator which is served up hot in the food court.

It is truly a remarkable and inspirational place that is largely powered by volunteers.

At the heart of the project is Jordan, a laid-back lover of life with a knack for motivating those around him. Well-wishers come to see how the festival stage is coming along, and find themselves mowing a field. Jordan is a natural leader, but not in a "Type A," "How to Motivate" sort of way. He merely exudes an energy that is contagious. And over the years he has deployed an army of workers.

Stages have been erected. Permits have been pulled. And in four short years a cultural institution has been built on the edge of our community.

I bumped into Jordan at the opening of the biodiesel plant. It was an enormous private party, with over five hundred supporters and Jordan, who is accustomed to thousands of overnight guests, was clearly impressed. He was grateful that we had brought biodiesel to town and said, "You guys look after the fuel. We'll take care of the entertainment."

That simple remark had a profound impact on me. Perhaps it was the afterglow of the speeches — or the conviviality of the evening, but it dawned on me that if we could each take our part of the load, we could form a self-reliant community that could exist without the need for massive external inputs.

From a business perspective, Jordan has been a long-time user of biodiesel. He buys off-road fuel from the Co-op. And he buys on-road fuel from Industrial. And in return, Piedmont Biofuels takes its tank truck out to the festival grounds every year so that people there can fill up with biodiesel. And it sponsors a booth in the "advocacy" part of the festival. Jordan buys a small quantity of fuel to power his mowers and his operation. And Piedmont buys an advertisement in his program that helps him offset his printing costs. Fuel gets traded for free weekend passes. These are small things.

One year, our musician in residence, Evan, fired up the Piedmont Biofuels String Band, and entered it into an open microphone event at Shakori. He recruited a handful of musicians from our project — some accomplished, some less so — and that band has been kicking around ever since.

Over the years the connection between the two properties has deepened. As a forward-thinking organization, Shakori offers free parking to anyone who comes in a full carload of people. Piedmont Biofuels is perpetually preaching fuel conservation and carpooling, and when they saw the Shakori policy in place, they reached out to get Frank to bring the "Biobus" out to the festival.

Frank is a baker from Durham who operates Ninth St. Bakery. Inspired by the biodiesel movement, he bought an immaculate Mercedes-Benz bus that had sat in a barn since the sixties. He filled it up with biodiesel, called it the "Biobus," and rents it out for events and special occasions.

Perhaps it was to popularize his bus, or perhaps it was because he was hip to the Shakori scene, or perhaps it was to form a closer tie with Piedmont, but for whatever reason, Frank started offering shuttle service from his bakery in downtown Durham to Shakori, and back again.

It is another small thing. Jordan sells a few more tickets to his show. Piedmont sells a little more fuel. There is one more public transportation option in the world. Maybe Frank takes in the show, or maybe his bus gets booked for an upcoming wedding. These are all the little transactions amongst ourselves that form the fiber of a sustainable community.

The other day Jordan stopped by Industrial for some fuel. He had a volunteer in tow, and clearly wanted to offer a "tour" of the biodiesel plant. We don't normally do impromptu tours, but my schedule was clear, it was a spring day and I wanted to be outside, so I walked around with Jordan and his guest. The plant was humming at full tilt. And we were shipping a lot of fuel.

"Have you made any money yet?" said Jordan.

"Nope. I'm thinking this will be the month," was my reply. "We're going to see our first black ink this April."

"And how about this weather?" I asked. "Let's ask the Cosmic Waiter for a seventy-degree weekend for this year's Shakori."

Jordan grinned; knowing that implicit in that request was big gate receipts and a massive turnout that is his ticket to profitability. "It looks like this will be the month for Chatham Marketplace," he remarked. And then he added, "Maybe April could be the one for all three."

It was a great thought. April 2007 could be the month of the triple bottom line. Instead of people, planet, profits, it could be Piedmont, Chatham Marketplace, and Shakori Hills.

A few nights later I encountered Jordan playing in a string band on the porch of Chatham Marketplace, which had implemented a new charitable giving program in which a percentage of the day's take is donated to one worthy cause. On this day, Shakori was that cause.

And the porch of the marketplace was jamming that night. I pulled in alone and ended up dining with the Mayor. Picnic tables were packed with music enthusiasts, and a cast party was underway on the porch.

Ellen and her husband, Ray, power the Pittsboro theatre scene in large part. She teaches drama at the community college, and has a habit of staging performances wherever she can. It might be a children's play in the multi-purpose room at the college, or she will sometimes grab space at Chatham Mills.

Ellen often teams up with singer-songwriter Drew Lasater to stage musicals. The two wrote, scored, and directed a play called *The Millworker* that received regional acclaim and went on to tour the state.

Whether they are setting *A Midsummer Night's Dream* in a twenties theme, or trying their hand at *One Flew Over the Cuckoo's Nest*, our thespian culture is alive and well. One of the remarkable things about the Pittsboro theater scene is that a nearby metropolis does not overshadow it. While our actors and actresses may not be professional, our community theatre is on par with that of nearby population centers. We lack space, but we are crowded with talent, and amazing plays are staged around town time and again.

Many small communities form on the edge of much greater centers. It is hard for a "little theatre" in Guelph, Ontario to get noticed in the shadow of Toronto. Yet little Pittsboro holds its own against the theatrical companies in the Triangle.

The same is true for the literary arts. One iconic business that often represents the last bastion of local business is the independent bookstore, and on that front, we have one. McIntyre's Fine Books and Bookends is in the heart of Fearrington Village, which is a quirky compact community on the north side of town. It's the brainchild of R. B. Fitch, and while it would be easy to characterize Fearrington as a golf-course community, it offers no golf. It is defined instead by the pet cows that graze around its entrance.

In the absence of golf, there is bocce. There are tennis courts, an outdoor swimming club, and croquet. And of course they offer garden size chess, on a set acquired from Moncure Chessworks.

In their faux town center they have a bank, a garden shop, a deli, and a restaurant. They have a toy shop, and others, and to the side of it all is a five-star restaurant where most of the staff speak with thick foreign accents. They have a country inn that is priced more for the honeymoon crowd than for the *Lonely Planet* traveler.

And they have a barn, which they use for readings, and plays, and speakers of all sorts. Fearrington is an unusual place with a Pittsboro address. It's not quite a town, it certainly doesn't like to be called a "retirement community," and it is the home of whole bunch of transplanted folks from up north who are more liberal-leaning than the local demographic, and more well-heeled as well. Fearrington's advertisements in the *New Yorker* appear to have paid off.

Fearrington residents tend to power our local charities, and volunteer boards, and tend to show up in our local schools as tutors and artists and influencers. It is a unique community asset, which asserts an interesting cultural opportunity for our town. When the local NPR affiliate is looking for a venue for a famous radio personality, they often chose Fearrington. When a famous author is making the rounds, they often chose McIntyre's, which uses the Fearrington Barn as a venue.

Local authors also use the Fearrington Barn, and we have our share of remarkable writers. *A Home on the Field* by Peruvian writer Paul Caudros was written here, as was Nancy Peacock's *Life Without Water*, Maggie Wilson's *Emma's Search for Grace*, and Marjorie Hudson's *Searching for Virginia Dare*. Marjorie has long been active in community life, and has led an effort to recognize the work of George Moses Horton, who was enslaved in Pittsboro and bought his freedom by selling poems on the streets of Chapel Hill.

Fearrington has hung its hat on folk art, and has installed a handful of Vollis Simpson pieces at its entranceway. He's the visionary from the other side of Zebulon who built a number of giant whirligigs around his pond — which the locals named "Acid Park." Vollis fastened hundreds of bicycle reflectors to the posts of his sculptures, causing an "acid trip" effect when approached at night. Each year Fearrington hosts a show which brings visionary outsider artists in from far and wide, and collectors of that genre converge on Pittsboro to make new acquisitions.

From a cultural perspective Chatham County is anchored by a vibrant visual arts community, complete with annual tour, and an active Arts Council, and by a growing sustainable agriculture community.

We can entertain ourselves. We don't need to leave town to do it. We might need to cross the lake to take in Eric Clapton, but it is easy to stumble across live music in Pittsboro. If not Shakori, then the General Store, if not the General Store then Chatham Marketplace, if not there, down at the biodiesel plant, if not there on the steps of Beggars and Choosers on a re-opening night.

It is entirely possible to be immersed in ideas, music, art, literature, and the stuff of culture without ever leaving town.

Healing Ourselves

Avoiding Big Fixes to Big Problems

ONE TIME TAMI AND I got all excited about medicinal herbs that we could grow about the place, so we ran off to Duke University to take a class. We planted horehound and Echinacea, and ginger and the usual suspects, and we read books and we studied and after we had surrounded ourselves with enough gardens to fill several medicine chests, we looked around for someone to cure.

No luck. We didn't have enough ailments to match our newfound knowledge. And as we waited for something to cure, we lost interest in the project. Most of our medicinal herbs have been abandoned or forgotten, swallowed up by honeysuckle, or Virginia creeper, or poison ivy, or any of the other invasive exotics which keep us surrounded at all times.

When Elizabeth Freedman came to town, and hung out her shingle, we had a chiropractor. She also performs acupuncture. She has one toe in traditional chiropractic care, and her heart in alternative healing modalities. She will also come to your office to evaluate your sitting posture, or the height of your workbench.

And we have a sliding scale clinic down the road in Moncure, which is unusual in this country, and is perhaps the most famous thing in Moncure. It's staffed by a bunch of well-intentioned doctors from the University of North Carolina, and it is generally so packed that it takes a vast portion of the day to get service.

We have a handful of dentists and we have a family medical practice that operates like the medical practice of my childhood. They will run an x-ray when you are having trouble breathing, and they will deliver babies, and they will set a cast for a broken arm. The usual.

They also know their patients by name, and follow the progress of generations. When Tami had Arlo she was laid up for six weeks in bed. She came home from the hospital with tubes inside and out, leaving me with Zafer, a rambunctious two-year-old, the newborn Arlo, and some bags on Tami that needed changing. And during this time, Dr. Tyler came to our house to help care for the infant.

I was raised in a small town in Ontario, where there is universal health coverage, and Dr. Butt would occasionally make house calls when we were too sick to get across town. Thirty-five years later in the woods of Chatham County, we can also get a house call when it is merited.

Once when Zafer had a seizure, so many first responders showed up at our house there was not enough room in the driveway. It must have been a slow night on the radio. I am still not sure why the dogcatcher arrived, but he did, and finding no place to park he pulled into my fledgling orchard and ran over one of my crabapple trees.

Dr. Tyler talks of the family medicine business as something that is becoming increasingly difficult. Big insurance companies and Health Maintenance Organizations have gained in strength over the years, and he has watched his practice go from keeping a dollar for services rendered to retaining only seventy cents. Nathan, who works as a physician's assistant over in Liberty laments about how the medical records of a lifetime once fit on a couple of pages of text, and now endless pages are required for each visit.

On the other side of town Dr. Garlick makes some astute observations about health care in our society. One day when he was taking a throat culture from me in search off strep throat, he remarked on how pigs have a more powerful constituency than humans do. "You can put in a hog farm with 100,000 animals and store their waste in a lagoon," he said. "If anyone suggests that might not be a good thing for public health, the idea is lost in the interest of raising more pigs."

Agriculture is more powerful than health care on Capitol Hill, and that fact shows up in our small-town doctor's offices.

Apart from traditional western healers, we have an abundance of massage therapists, thanks in large part to the Body Therapy Institute in Silk Hope, and we have a wide selection of alternative health care practitioners. From crystals to aromatherapy to energy work performed with magic wands, we are covered. From Feldenkrais to colonics to yoga and back again our woods are filled with healers.

Down in Mt. Vernon, twenty minutes to the other side of the county, we have the famous Mt. Vernon Springs. One is for health, and one is for beauty, and both attract lineups of cars.

The time I took a milk jug down to Mt. Vernon springs I had to wait my turn. I only had one jug, so I filled from the health spring — feeling I was fine as far as beauty was concerned. And when I took a slug from the bottle, I was stunned that people collected this water at all. It tasted like metal. It was nasty. Not far from the site is an historical marker that commemorates a famous iron mine which provided valuable material to the Confederate army.

It all made me think I know very little about healing ourselves.

I had a fascinating look into the health of humans one day
at a Burlington Town Council meeting. I was there to get approval for the opening of a biodiesel pump in their small town,
and since my agenda item was at the end of the list, I had to sit
through a bunch of other mind-numbing town business. Everything from proclamations to awards to the announcement of
the Mayor's support for National Public Works Week.

On first blush I found myself re-evaluating my life. Had
I really worked so hard lo these many years to find myself in
the chambers of the Burlington Town Council celebrating National Public Works Week? Yet when Gary Hicks, the Director
of Public Works took the podium, he made some interesting
remarks. He had put his staff on a "wellness" program that involved early detection checkups and preventative health care
measures, and he was noting to the councilors how successful
the program had been.

"We've been doing this for our buses for years," he said. "It's
about time we did it for our employees."

Our town has a couple of generations of dentists, and the
preventative aspect of dental care also applies. I once took a
history course at the University of Western Ontario where I
learned that with the invention of dentistry the general level
of violence in society dropped. Apparently one of the reasons
the grizzly bear is a more dangerous animal than his black bear
cousins is because of its teeth. And it is true that when your
teeth hurt, your whole life hurts.

⬡⬡⬡

I suppose the best answer to whether or not we could maintain
our health in our small town setting depends on a wide variety
of variables, including luck. Maintaining good health is easier

than fighting back to good health when good health has been lost, and we are well positioned to maintain good health, depending on which literature people believe.

I am a giant fan of Michael Pollan, the author of *Omnivore's Dilemma*, who has delved deeply into the problem with our national state of health lying in what he calls "nutritionism." Because it is politically impossible to take on unhealthy constituencies, nutritional science has emerged to attack certain attributes of food on the basis of health. Instead of telling consumers to eat less red meat, for instance, we are told to "reduce our cholesterol."

For Pollan, nutritionism is a philosophy to which we have all come to subscribe. It says "statens bad," or "anti-oxidants good," which leads to fad after fad in the way we eat. From wheat germ to oat bran to red wine to fat in to fat out to reduced carbohydrates, American eaters jump from one nutritional claim to the next, the whole time ignoring the fact that what we really need to do is eat "whole food." Real food. And I would add "local food." The flora in our guts will take what it needs to stay healthy, given the chance, and what it needs is whole food.

Which has nothing to do with the heroics we have come to demand of our health care system. When it is our loved one, we demand a perfect outcome every time, which means we prefer life flights on helicopters bound for specialized facilities — the mere existence of which demands a certain concentrated size.

It would not have been OK for Tami to have died giving birth to Arlo. We have midwives and doulas who provide vastly superior birthing experiences to those on offer in our regional hospitals, but they may not have been helpful enough for the ruptured uterus and torn bladder that came along with Arlo.

And the same competitive notion that afflicts education is evident in our health care system. I once attended a forum on economic development that was being facilitated by our

Economic Development Corporation. Someone mentioned the need for better medical care for our aging population, to which the people at the hospital in Siler City objected. "Let's make sure that any new services we dream up do not compete with services which are already there."

Once again the conversation is couched in competition. But we can also cooperate. Our species is adept at doing both. And it could be that it is through cooperation that we might expand our service level, using existing investments like the hospital in Siler City.

At the end of the day the fundamental healing that needs to go on is in our heads. We have a good supply of therapists on hand, although I believe that if everyone started going to therapy as much as they should — just to get to a basic minimum maintenance level — we would run out of shrinks awfully fast.

If we could find a comfort level with the quantity of stuff we have, we would rapidly find ourselves needing less stuff. And the same is true of money. And fuel. And food. If we could change our collective self-image from one of "consumers" to "conservers," we would need to do a whole lot less healing in the first place.

I like the thinking of Craig Venter on this subject. He's the one who led the private sector's effort to sequence the human genome, and who published the work for all to use.

One of his core arguments for untangling our genetic maps is that it could lead a preventative approach to health care. He laments that we do not live in a "preventative society," and that we prefer "big fixes to big problems."

I once took a tour of a wastewater treatment plant, in which all of the sewage of Chapel Hill was pouring in one side, and there were fish swimming in the treated effluent that was coming out the other. It was group tour, and I lost interest in the technical details, so I struck up a conversation with one of the administrators. I was intrigued to learn that his relationship to water was very similar to my relationship to fuel. The average Chapel Hill resident consumes about eight thousand gallons of water each month. He was proud of the fact that his household of four residents (including two teenage daughters) was six thousand gallons a month.

I remarked that my daughters tended to go through the water whenever they were in town, and he shrugged. "One of them starts taking a long shower, I beat on the door and shout 'You're making University Lake go dry,' and that usually does the trick."

He had the self image of a conserver. His daily job is to ensure the public health of everything downstream — including Lake Jordan, where much of our drinking water comes from.

And it is interesting how conservation might take hold of one area of our lives, but not another. I remember once going to lunch in my brother Glen's Honda Insight. It was one of the first hybrid engines on the market. We were meeting with the primary author of the state's solar tax credits — a solar guru renowned throughout the land. He showed up in an SUV. He clearly understood electrical conservation through and through, but had not transferred his enthusiasm over to fuel conservation.

I'm the same way. I'm pathologically obsessed with fuel conservation, generally annoying on the subject of electricity conservation, and largely oblivious when it comes to clean water.

The path to sustainability lies in the conservation. That is by far the largest resource remaining to us, and it is the one that does the least harm when it is consumed. If we really want to heal ourselves, we need to start by shrinking all of our footprints dramatically.

Healing, like fueling and feeding, is much easier to do when there is less of it required.

Governing Ourselves

From Dirty Tricks to Soft Consensus

W HEN I WAS KID my mother always used to say, "Govern yourself accordingly."

That was a lofty expression for a little boy. But I figured it was fine, since my father worked at a control valve company called Fisher Governor. His products governed flow rates, and she was interested in how her children governed themselves, so it all made sense.

Our political world is strange indeed. We once had a County Commissioner named Bunkey Morgan who lived a long way away. If you are going to serve the people of Chatham County, you are supposed to live in Chatham County, but Bunkey had another vision. He was backed by a whole bunch of money from out-of-town developers and when he and his cronies took power a whole lot of our world suddenly changed. The Land Use Plan that was carefully crafted by concerned volunteer citizens landed in the shredder, the planning board recommendations were thrown to the wind, and in one short term our county became the purview of golf course developers.

The architects of Bunkey's success were very smart. They realized that in order to win the board they would need to run as Democrats, and in order to win as Democrats they would need to win in the primary. Win the primary, walk into power virtually uncontested in Chatham County. So Bunkey became a Democrat, and stomped our beloved left-leaning Shakori preaching Gary Phillips who used to run things around here.

But Bunkey's term awakened a new beast.

Jeffrey Starkweather and the dormant left awoke to form the Chatham Coalition, a grassroots political action committee that started knocking on doors and holding forums and mailing out flyers. They deployed listservs and websites and sign campaigns and they went about winning elections. In fact their candidates have won on three out of the last three occasions, and they have started behaving like a machine.

I'm pro-machine. The only thing I don't like about their behavior is they have the habit of slamming me whenever I disagree with them in the press. Dare I suggest they have made a horrible mistake; I get spanked within an inch of my life.

Which doesn't tend to stop me.

I've held fundraisers for the machine, I've donated money to the machine, and I am pro machine.

But there is the problem of dissent. Once when I found myself in a raging dispute with the good people of the Kenan Flagler Business School at the University of North Carolina, one of their people quipped that it was a shame that the left always arranges its firing squads in a circle. We seem less able to "stay on message," more inclined to question ideas, and less likely to maintain a united front.

In the grassroots community, consensus is a popular decision-making technique. Once everyone is on board with a decision, we roll. Consensus can be slow, and can require "the talking stick," which I have seen used many times in groups around town. Only the one holding the stick is allowed to speak, making room for the quiet types to have equal time with the loudmouths in the group.

At Piedmont Biofuels we operate on "soft consensus," which means that if you don't have an opinion on a decision, you stay out of the debate.

The Haw River Assembly, which has been advocating on behalf of our watershed for the past twenty-five years, and has become a powerful and entrenched voice in our environmental community, refers to its process as "empowerment through chaos." The Haw River Assembly is known for being fleet of foot. They get things done. From the festival they stage each year, which includes taking kids down the Haw River on overnight camping trips in canoes, to the "Stream Watch" program which they administer — they are a steadfast and powerful voice for environmental activism in our region.

Chatham Marketplace, on the other hand, has strict board governance guidelines they adhere to. It takes them a month to do the annual review of their general manager.

And Chatham County's governmental process is even worse. Our machine once appointed me to our Green Building Task Force. Alicia Ravetto, the architect, chaired it. She had the brilliant idea of setting each meeting on the first Monday of every month, and holding each meeting in a different location.

We started out in the dingy, florescent-lit room of our government's agricultural building, and Alicia was eager to move the meeting to the RAFI building, a daylit masterpiece with Energy Star certification. Then she was going to hold the meeting at the EMJ building, which is the largest commercial geothermal installation in North Carolina, and boasts a number of other green building features. The next would be held down at Piedmont Biofuels, where the rule is that everyone gets daylight and fresh air.

But she was unable to move the meetings around for fear of violating the "Public Meetings Law," which is designed to let the public know where and when meetings are in advance, so that they can attend. No one from the public has ever attended a meeting of the Green Building Task Force, and on most nights, most of the appointees fail to show up as well, but government runs as government runs.

As we enter our second year of monthly meetings, we find ourselves with a compromise. Each meeting is held in the conference room of the RAFI building — much better than the basement where we began — but we are largely unable to change venues.

One of the groups that has sprung up in our midst is Chatham Citizens for Effective Communities (CCEC). Apart from sending emissaries to endless public meetings, and reporting back on their website, they have also sponsored a "Governing School," in which they explain how our local government works. Each semester they turn out a new crop of twenty to thirty "graduates," many of whom take positions on the county's many advisory boards. The program is the brain child of Rita Spina, a powerhouse of ideas out in Fearrington Village. If the Chatham Coalition is a political action committee for a progressive agenda, then CCEC could be considered a progressive watchdog group. And teaching "civics" appears to be an effective way to increase civic participation.

One of the outcomes of the new political regime is a moratorium on growth. Woven into the fabric of our new leadership is a deep desire to provide "smart growth." And today in our environment, smart growth means "more study." Which means a moratorium is a way to buy time. Our community is up against powerful forces, many of which have more resources than us. I once stopped by Town Hall only to trip over a mountain of boxes that had been dropped off by a Raleigh developer. Across the top of each was a giant sticker that read, "Litigation Grade Documents." Nice hint. I felt confident that our Town Planner, Dave Monroe, would be unfazed by such a thing. He's whipped powerful forces in the past, and we are in good hands with him around.

⬡⬡⬡

One way to limit growth is to limit infrastructure, and that is a strategy that has been pursued by our Town Fathers in the past. Pittsboro operates an antiquated wastewater system, which discharges into Roberson Creek and finds its way to Jordan Lake. Since the wastewater plant is undersized and obsolete, it routinely discharges raw sewage during rain events. As a result the plant is just as routinely out of compliance with State regulations.

Once upon a time in Pittsboro the political decision was made that there would be no upgrade or investment in wastewater required. It may have been a town board who liked Pittsboro just the way it was and had no desire to see it change. The decision meant no increases in taxes or water and sewer rates, and it meant the town could remain small. When the plant repeatedly failed, the State took away Pittsboro's wastewater growth options, a moratorium on new sewer connections was imposed by the state and we have stayed small as a result.

In Chapel Hill, on the other hand, they just finished their fifty-million-dollar upgrade on their system. With their eyes wide open to the increased rates for water and sewer that would need to be passed along to the users of the system, they elected to pay a premium for their spotless effluent.

We could do that too. And the ability to handle wastewater would cause our town to explode. In the absence of such an investment, we stay small. A danger of staying small is that giant developers will simply build state of the art waste treatment facilities that are superior to ours. We can decide if we want our utilities to be privately held by real estate interests, or publicly controlled by our government — which is supposed to be us.

⬡⬡⬡

It is too bad we can't govern by "buzz."

People move here because they have heard the buzz about the sustainable agriculture which is going on down at the college. Or because they can join the biodiesel co-op. Or because of our remarkable co-op grocery store. Or because of the farmers' market. Land is still affordable, and Pittsboro has a lot of gravitational pull. One of the problems we have around town is that when someone says "I'll meet you at the Co-op," we don't know which location they are talking about.

Cooperatives are a form of governance. Chatham Marketplace and Piedmont Biofuels are both "consumer co-ops," which means people buy memberships in order to gain access to the products that are for sale.

At Chatham Marketplace, the ownership fee is a one-time charge. Co-op owners might one day get a "dividend" back that is based on purchases. Ownerships are refundable if you move away, but they are required for you to vote in board elections.

Piedmont Biofuels, on the other hand, does not offer refundable memberships. It's fifty dollars a year for as long as the member wishes to buy fuel. There are no cash "dividends."

Richard Heinberg, author of *Power Down*, and other "energy" books, has put out the concept of lifeboats. For him, lifeboats are those projects that might survive in a resource-depleted future. Heinberg fans like to point to Piedmont Biofuels as a lifeboat project. Our preference would be to avoid the dark future Heinberg writes about, but if he is seeing the inevitable, I suppose we will take the lifeboat label.

When we survey Pittsboro, we spot a number of lifeboat projects, and on close examination, they are all governed differently. Blue Heron, our co-housing community, is "process intensive," with a talking stick and complete buy-in from members of the community. Our Land Lab down at the Community College could be described as a lifeboat project, since it is instrumental in kicking out both food and knowledge into the community — and it is governed by a Community College System, which has governance assigned by the State.

And Piedmont Biofuels has a number of governing strategies. The Co-op is governed by a volunteer board, which is elected by the membership. Shareholders — along the same lines as corporations everywhere — govern Industrial. En masse, we probably lean toward the Haw River Assembly model, with chaotic governance, yet high results.

Which makes me think that putting energy into governing methodology might just be a waste of energy. Presumably, the Cold War was fought over differences in governing strategies, which is about on par with the wars of the Lilliputians. Whether we open our eggs from the little end or the big end is not the point. The point is to successfully get at the egg itself.

I'm guessing there are flaws in all forms of governance. When Cuba lost its subsidized petroleum with the collapse of the Soviet Union, they converted their economy to sustainable agriculture. The loss of petroleum inputs into agriculture caused birth weights to drop, and malnutrition to set in. Cubans took to the ditches to plant row crops, and chicken coops appeared in high rises, and farmers' markets showed up on street corners, and miraculously, Cuba figured out how to feed itself.

It should be noted that it was the Cuban people, not the government, who led the charge on their way into sustainable agriculture.

There is a documentary called *The Power of Community: How Cuba Survived Peak Oil*. It is a completely inspirational tale about what is possible. Once the farm at the biodiesel co-op was out of arable land, and since I had some amazing soil, and a good water source, and an endless market, I decided to erect a deer fence. When I was done I called it "Cuba," and Emily put in a crop of sweet potatoes and eggplants, and the children and I took off a crop of popcorn.

Cuba, under a communist government, figured out how to feed itself in the absence of petroleum. The United States is a democracy that has not had to face that particular problem. In Cuba, where the eggs come from the rooftop above, people are imprisoned for criticizing government. In the United States, where eggs are plentiful and cheap, and where people are free to throw barbs at their government, people are imprisoned for being terrorists. And we ship the terrorists to our naval base in Cuba.

Whether it is Robert's Rules of Order, Empowerment through Chaos, meetings governed by "Public Meeting Laws," or back room deals done in the night is not the point. The point is that the good work needs to get done.

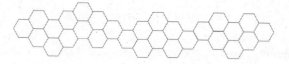

Conclusion

Life's Big Adventure

I ONCE SPENT A WEEKEND with my boys, my dear friend Gary, and his children, Sage and Giles. We attempted to stay organized. We loaded up with pickaxes and shovels and headed to a rock outcropping near Wake Forest in search of garnet stones. Along the way we stopped at a typical chain roadhouse for lunch.

I analyzed everyone's order, from the perspective of my "hundred mile diet," thereby ruining everybody's meal. Whether it was the preservative-laden lettuce, the petroleum in the cheese sticks, and the antibiotic in the hamburger — I laid out the usual criticisms of a typical American meal at a typical American restaurant.

After loading up on garnet stones, we stopped at a go-cart racetrack where we played video games, and took shifts in batting cages, and raced around what was essentially a small amusement park.

And I was bored out of my head. I was once a connoisseur of video games. I once dreamt of racing go-carts. And yet I was utterly underwhelmed by the experience. Gary, on the other hand, was jazzed.

The next morning I served up a breakfast spread and identified where every ingredient had come from. Eggs from Judy Hogan, sausage from Cane Creek, herbs from the backyard garden, and so on. I'm guessing the children are largely uninterested in my "local food" tirades — they are after all, largely "pastatarians," with poorly developed palates.

But after the weekend I headed off to Quack and Back and explored my boredom with John. He framed it as if we are engaged in a video game. The rules are simple. Try to find a way to sustain human life on earth. When you are in the game, it is easy to get up in the morning and start playing with everything you've got. I believe it was Scott Nearing who wrote, "Find work that you love and you will never work again," and that dictum lies at the heart of many of our projects.

Like John, Sally is a well known therapist in these parts, who has turned her energy to film making.

I attended the premiere of *What A Way to Go: Life at the End of Empire*, which is an intriguing film by Sally Erickson and her partner, Tim Bennett. It is an intense and gloomy piece of work in its analysis of the human condition, and it is a straight-ahead look at what humans have done to our nest.

In the discussion that followed, the concept of "community" arose, and one commenter suggested that "there is no community — there is no one to look after you." It was a bleak statement. We rode home with Greg, one of the fuel makers at Piedmont, and in our discussion of the movie we found the opposite to be true.

Resource depletion, societal collapse, and impending doom may just be the best thing that ever happened to "community."

The night before the premiere, we had all attended a housewarming party at David's new home. He spearheads the design-build work at Piedmont Biofuels. The party over-flowed his property. There were potters and educators, artists and musicians, herbalists and store clerks. There were policy makers and researchers and wetlands consultants. And a common thread, which ran through them all, was a keen interest in sustainability.

I didn't manage to speak to everyone at the party, and the next morning, I thought of a half-dozen people whom I would have loved to have talked to — but missed because the event was too large. And I thought about David's new home. It had been abandoned. Then renovated, then abandoned again. For most of my time in the neighborhood it has been empty. To see it overflowing with interesting people was a treat.

It occurred to me that our community has never been stronger. Ten years ago, if I needed a ride to town, I would have found myself stranded in the woods. Today I could catch a half dozen rides — and none of them would be "out of the way." Today there are more people "looking after" one another than ever before.

We once had an intern come unraveled in a manic episode that made him a candidate for twenty-four hour care. And we took shifts, around the clock, for three days, until his family arrived from afar. Whether you need the garden watered, or a pet cared for, or a safe place to heal, or a ride to town, these woods have never been so full of opportunities.

Or full of so many people who are on life's big adventure.

Surely there are some who are still trapped in their Prius's, burning a couple of hours each day in an effort to earn enough money to sustain their little chunk of paradise.

And when these folks are at the party, surrounded by those who are powered by passion, and completely jazzed by working at what they love, they may question the lives they have carved out for themselves.

I often ask Gary when he is going to abandon his commute, and his livelihood, and jump in on Life's Big Adventure — doing something that is infused with daily meaning. He plays with the idea. We need as many new players as we can get.

And it turns out those who are fully engaged in the game tend to lose their desire to drive a go-cart around a circular track.

Bibliography

Bennet, Tim, and Erickson, Sally. *What a Way to Go: Life at the End of Empire*. Vision Quest Pictures, 2006.

Estill, Lyle. *Biodiesel Power: The Passion, the People and the Politics of the Next Renewable Fuel*. New Society, 2007.

Estill, Lyle. Energy Blog. biofuels.coop. Piedmont Biofuels, 2003.

Heinberg, Richard. *Power Down: Options and Actions for a Post-Carbon World*. New Society, 2004.

Hudson, Marjorie. *Searching for Virginia Dare: A Fool's Errand*. Coastal Carolina Press, 2002.

Kaufman, Wallace. *Coming Out of the Woods: The Solitary Life of a Maverick Naturalist*. Perseus Publishing, 2000.

Keillor, Garrison. *A Prairie Home Companion*. National Public Radio.

Korten, David. *The Great Turning: From Empire to Earth Community*. People-Centered Development Forum, 2006.

Kunstler, James. *The Long Emergency: Surviving the Converging Catastrophes of the Twenty-First Century*. Atlantic Monthly Press, 2005

Leacock, Stephen. *Sunshine Sketches of a Little Town*. Broadview Press, 2002.

Lovins, Amory. *Small is Profitable: The Hidden Economic Benefits of Making Electrical Resources the Right Size*. Rocky Mountain Institute, 2002.

McLuhan, Marshall. *The Global Village: Transformations in World Life and Media in the 21st Century*. Oxford University Press, 1992.

McRobie, George. *Small is Possible*. Harper and Row Publishers, 1981.

Morgan, Faith. *The Power of Community: How Cuba Survived Peak Oil*. The Community Solution, 2006.

Nearing, Helen and Scott. *Living the Good Life*. Schocken Books Inc., 1970

Pahl, Greg. *Citizen Powered Community Handbook: Community Solutions to a Global Crisis*. Chelsea Green, 2007.

Peacock, Nancy. *Life Without Water*. Bantam Books, 1998.

Peck, Scott. *The Different Drum: Community Making and Peace*. Touchstone, 1987.

Perkins, John. *Confessions of an Economic Hit Man*. Berrett-Koehler Publishers, Inc. 2004.

Pollan, Michael. *The Omnivore's Dilemma: A Natural History of Four Meals*. The Penguin Press, 2006.

Raymond, Steven. *The Cathedral and the Bazaar: Musings on Linux and Open Source by an Accidental Revolutionary*. O'Reilly Publications, 1999.

Schumacher, E.F. *Small is Beautiful: Economics as if People Mattered*. Harper Perennial, 1973.

Schultz, Mark, ed. *Chapel Hill News*. News and Observer, 2007

Sereno, Julian, ed. *Chatham County Line*, Chatham County Line Publishers, 2007.

Shuman, Michael. *Going Local: Creating Self-Reliant Communities in a Global Age*. The Free Press, 1998.

Shuman, Michael. *The Small-Mart Revolution: How Local Businesses are Beating the Global Competition*. Berrett-Koehler Publishers, Inc., 2006.

Twain, Mark, *Life on the Mississippi*. Modern Library, 2007.

Wilson, Maggie. *Emma's Search for Grace*. Wilson Ink, 2004.

Index

About the Author

Photo credit: Tami Schwerin

Lyle Estill has been writing at his kitchen table in the woods of Chatham County, North Carolina, since September 2003. Before that he wrote in the laundry room of his place in Raleigh, North Carolina, and in the attic of his house in Guelph, Ontario. For awhile he wrote in his brother's basement in London, Ontario, and before that he wrote a novel on the front porch of his other brother's place in Fredericton, New Brunswick. When he lived in Fisher Branch, Manitoba, he wrote in the living room.

He started out as a journalist, switched to short fiction, abandoned that for poetry, went back to news-editorial, changed over to commentary, and now writes mostly blog entries, newspaper columns, and magazine articles. He's been publishing stuff since 1979.

These days Estill is a self styled sustainability enthusiast, who pursues local food and days on his front porch with an almost religious fervor.

If you have enjoyed *Small is Possible*, you might also enjoy other

Books to Build a New Society

Our books provide positive solutions for people who want to make a difference. We specialize in:

Sustainable Living ✦ Ecological Design and Planning
Natural Building & Appropriate Technology ✦ New Forestry
Environment and Justice ✦ Conscientious Commerce
Progressive Leadership ✦ Resistance and Community ✦ Nonviolence
Educational and Parenting Resources

New Society Publishers

ENVIRONMENTAL BENEFITS STATEMENT

New Society Publishers has chosen to produce this book on recycled paper made with 100% post consumer waste, processed chlorine free, and old growth free.

For every 5,000 books printed, New Society saves the following resources:[1]

21	Trees
1,894	Pounds of Solid Waste
2,084	Gallons of Water
2,718	Kilowatt Hours of Electricity
3,443	Pounds of Greenhouse Gases
15	Pounds of HAPs, VOCs, and AOX Combined
5	Cubic Yards of Landfill Space

---

[1]Environmental benefits are calculated based on research done by the Environmental Defense Fund and other members of the Paper Task Force who study the environmental impacts of the paper industry.

For a full list of NSP's titles, please call 1-800-567-6772 or check out our web site at:

www.newsociety.com

NEW SOCIETY PUBLISHERS